Small Business Total Quality

Small Business Total Quality

Neil Huxtable

Peratec Limited
Swindon
UK

CHAPMAN & HALL

London · Glasgow · Weinheim · New York · Tokyo · Melbourne · Madras

**Published by Chapman & Hall, 2–6 Boundary Row,
London SE1 8HN, UK**

Chapman & Hall, 2–6 Boundary Row, London SE1 8HN, UK

Blackie Academic & Professional, Wester Cleddens Road, Bishopbriggs,
Glasgow G64 2NZ, UK

Chapman & Hall GmbH, Pappelallee 3, 69469 Weinheim, Germany

Chapman & Hall USA, One Penn Plaza, 41st Floor,
New York NY 10119, USA

Chapman & Hall Japan, ITP-Japan, Kyowa Building, 3F, 2-2-1
Hirakawacho, Chiyoda-ku, Tokyo 102, Japan

Chapman & Hall Australia, Thomas Nelson Australia, 102 Dodds Street,
South Melbourne, Victoria 3205, Australia

Chapman & Hall India, R. Seshadri, 32 Second Main Road, CIT East,
Madras 600 035, India

First edition 1995

© 1995 Neil Huxtable

Typeset in Times 11/13pts by Mews Photosetting, Beckenham, Kent
Printed in Great Britain by Hartnolls Ltd, Bodmin, Cornwall

ISBN 0 412 60270 9

A catalogue record for this book is available from the British Library

Library of Congress Catalog Card Number: 94-72664

I FY MEIBION
ALED A GERAINT

Contents

Foreword

Paul Spenley: Director
Peratec

The ability to implement best practice methods and techniques into any company is paramount in achieving and maintaining the competitive edge required to ensure profitable operation.

To help achieve this objective, there are many so-called panaceas often put forward by people with no practical experience of business. As a result of this, the ideas propounded sound wonderful, but practical guidance required to implement best practice in the real world is often overlooked.

Total Quality is quite simply best practice in common sense, and in this book the approach is specifically aimed at helping small and medium-sized businesses.

The author has a real understanding and feel for small/medium company issues and culture and for the first time, here is a TQM book which is specifically aimed at providing practical help to all of these businesses.

Introduction

The principles of Total Quality Management (TQM) are now a recognized characteristic of most successful businesses. Customer demands, the awesome penetration of Japan and its Pacific rim neighbours into Western markets and the need for stringent cost management in fluctuating economic environments make TQM a practice of paramount importance for every enterprise, big or small. Gone are the days when customers considered price as the main reason for purchasing a product or service. Quality and reliability are now the overriding factors which customers favour in exercising choice. Meeting customer specification, dependability of service and speed of delivery are the very distinguishing features of success. No other theory of business management addresses these issues more fully than TQM.

TQM, however, is a complex issue. There are many examples both within the United Kingdom, Western Europe and the United States of its successful introduction. Indeed Japanese investment within these countries has proved TQM's adaptability, giving the lie to the view that it is inextricably coupled to an Eastern work ethic and culture. Western workers can be as successful as their far Eastern counterparts in achieving the possibilities to be realized from a focus on Total Quality. (Ironically TQM was a Western concept exported to the East after the Second World War when spurned by Western industrialists as impracticable.)

However, even with overwhelming evidence to the contrary, many companies have failed in their attempts to realize the benefits of TQM. This has been borne out by a number of industrial surveys which show that lack of sustained commitment by senior management or inadequate planning have often contributed to a shortfall in the business results hoped for from TQM initiatives. Other causes of failure include the inability to change, failure to identify and satisfy true customer needs or to progress beyond registration to quality standards BS 5750/ISO 9000.

The prospect of implementing a TQM drive, where much larger companies have failed, must prove daunting for smaller businesses where the lack of resources, if not the motivation, could easily impede the implementation of such a fundamental change.

Despite this, large organizations are placing more and more demands upon their suppliers – many of whom are small family-run businesses – for first-class quality. Moreover, many small businesses, wooed no doubt by government grants and national advertising campaigns, have responded by acquiring BS 5750 or its European (EN 29000) and international (ISO 9000) equivalents. For many companies quality stops here. However, as more and more companies obtain the standard BS 5750 accreditation is no longer enough. Large companies are asking their suppliers to go beyond BS 5750. They expect increased quality and reduced prices – in other words the implementation of full Total Quality. As a result I have realized for some time that there is a real need for a practical handbook for smaller companies that will give particular advice on how to introduce Total Quality Management.

This book is designed to meet that need. It should assist all small businesses from those employing a mere handful of people to companies of a hundred or more staff. It should help both BS 5750 registered small companies and also serves as a practical guide for those companies that have made no attempt to introduce any formal process of quality improvement. It places quality assurance and BS 5750/ISO 9000 registration in its rightful place within the quality improvement process. It also lays great stress on the need for cost control and cashflow management, two crucial areas for a small organization. Other elements include a company-wide view of customer care with an emphasis on employee care as a prerequisite for all successful customer care programmes. It stresses the critical importance of leadership and company culture, matters which can often come under strain as small businesses expand, jeopardizing the 'personal touch' which has frequently marked their earlier success. The book discusses the 'empowerment' of the workforce to achieve a successful business that will satisfy the very highest expectations set. Also explored is the importance of business processes and a team-based approach to problem-solving, revealing them as key milestones along the route to continuous improvement and customer satisfaction. I have not written a specific chapter on the subject of communications. In view of its overriding importance throughout the TQM process, I have made specific references to the matter in the context of other issues as and when considered.

Small Business Total Quality is intended to give practical help and early results. It does not labour big-company TQM problems but offers best practice guidelines which will place any small organization, whether in the manufacturing or service sector, on a course of continuous improvement. It will be of benefit to both owners and senior managers of small enterprises as well as being a useful guide in demystifying the aura of TQM for supervisors and shop-floor employees.

Owing to the general introductory nature of this book, I have not explored in any great depth some of the more complex or specialized statistical or production techniques such as statistical process control (SPC), quality function deployment (QFD) or just-in-time manufacturing (JIT). I have made reference to these subjects where relevant and have usually referred the reader to in-depth sources of information should they be subjects of particular importance or interest.

In terms of layout, each chapter subject has been arranged in accordance to a number of relevant subheadings and concludes with a series of summary points. Many case studies of the successful implementation of TQM within small companies are included to stimulate small business managers to initiate or persevere with TQM. I have also included case studies from larger organizations where the size of the organization is irrelevant in the illustration of a particular point. A guide to the use of this book has been added to enable readers to gain ready access to particular concerns. I have also included sources of further information in the appendices. In particular information on the many Quality awards now available to companies demonstrating excellence in TQM may be obtained from the British Quality Foundation and the European Foundation for Quality Management, details of which are contained in Appendix D.

Two textual points worthy of note are the use of the term 'small business manager' as a generic description of the small business entrepreneur, owner or senior manager and, for the sake of convenience and without wishing to encourage any sexist overtones, the use where necessary of the masculine form of the third person personal pronoun throughout.

In conclusion, I would like to thank my consultancy colleagues for being a source of frequent advice and suggestion without whose encouragement, not to mention coercion at times, the completion of this book would have become a more arduous task to realize.

How to use this book

Potential readers of this book may fall into a number of different categories. Some no doubt will be fully versed in the theory of TQM but have as yet not commenced implementation, others will have introduced elements of TQM without possessing a clear idea of how it all fits together. Still more may be experiencing problems which they would like a TQM approach to address. The following matrix is designed to assist different categories of reader to gain maximum benefit from the book in dealing with issues affecting their business.

Reader requirement	Relevant sections
Full understanding of TQM	The whole book
TQM planning	Chapters 3, 4, 5, 6 and 12
Development of the management team	Chapters 3, 7, 8 and 12
Getting the most out of the work force	Chapters 6, 7, 8 and 12
Cost savings	Chapter 5
Supplier relations	Chapter 6
Improving customer satisfaction	Chapters 4 and 6
BS5750/ISO 9000 registration	Chapters 2 and 10
Problem solving	Chapter 9 and Appendix B
TQM implementation	Chapter 12

PART ONE

Background to
Total Quality

The small business in context

1.1 INTRODUCTION

Throughout Europe economies are to a large extent dependent on the success of the small business sector. In the United Kingdom alone more than 70% of all companies employ under 100 people. If economies are to prosper then it is essential that this sector remains vibrant.

Many small businesses are family-run concerns, perhaps passed down through a number of generations. Others will be newly formed or be experiencing rapid growth as a result of the skills and energy of their entrepreneur founders. Nevertheless in the face of global competition and ever increasing customer demands, the small business sector must demonstrate the business acumen of its larger international competitors to survive.

Market economies have also witnessed a breakup of many state monopolies. Government functions, traditionally hierarchical and offering long-term careers to their employees, are no longer in evidence. In order to stimulate their economies many governments at both national and local level are privatizing their traditional functions, fragmenting them into smaller businesses and in the process exposing them to competition from the commercial sectors. Jobs for life are no longer available. We all must become sensitive to the needs of our customers and the threat of competition if we wish to remain in employment.

Many small businesses with a turnover of under half a million pounds and employing up to, say, 15 people very often only have one particular product or service. They are therefore very vulnerable to shifts in market trends. Such companies can find themselves frequently exposed if they don't continually satisfy customer needs or adapt to shifting market trends.

1.2 CHARACTERISTICS OF THE SMALL BUSINESS

Despite this potentially gloomy picture, small businesses have a number of advantages over their larger competitors. Flexibility and speed of response often far exceed the capabilities of larger organizations. The flair of the entrepreneur or the success of a family in ownership often instils great staff loyalty and hard work. The personal commitment of the owner of a small business creates a cohesion and enhanced common purpose amongst the workforce which, if exploited wisely, can result in smaller organizations being able to match or exceed larger rivals in satisfying customer requirements.

However, as businesses grow so problems can ensue. Many businesses go through distinct phases in their development (Figure 1.1). They often commence on a product-drive basis. This occurs where the particular expertise of the founder has been exploited to create a business. He or she usually possesses greater skills than the staff which are employed and is looked up to as a source of insight and rare knowledge. Businesses of this nature very frequently

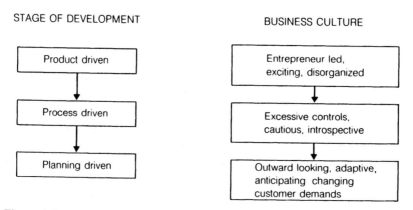

Figure 1.1 The business development process.

prove successful. However, in the development of an organization this stage will only be transitory. There are few businesses able to grow successfully while remaining dependent on a limited product range and the technical expertise of the founder alone. Those product-driven companies which remain static, perhaps through the exploitation of a niche market, will eventually be subject to competition which could expose their shortcomings or threaten their very existence.

The second phase of development – sometimes referred to as the process driven stage – occurs where a business has grown from its initial product-driven success. Businesses operating within this phase of development apply controls of various types, quality control in particular, perhaps as a result of a bad experience with a particular customer or changing customer requirements. The small business manager is no longer able to manage personally every facet of his or her business owing to its size and complexity. As a result everything must be checked before it leaves the organization. Frustrations amongst staff may ensue as excess checking, over-management and a spirit of caution dampens the enthusiasm and morale once evident at the firm's incipiency.

Firms which manage to pass through this introspective stage in their development enter a more expansive stage of growth – the planning-drive phase. This occurs when a small business has reached sufficient maturity to enable its management to plan ahead, looking beyond the confines of the business, anticipating changing customer demands and developing particular strategies to meet them.

1.3 THE FAMILY FIRM

Apart from newly founded businesses, the other main type of organization prevalent within the small business sector is the family firm. These may be relatively new organizations or companies of long standing where control has remained within the same family for a number of generations. Family businesses can become very successful – Sainsbury, Marks & Spencer, Pilkington and Laura Ashley are all examples of family companies which have achieved great success. Commitment of family members, staff loyalty and a particular work ethic are all factors which lay in favour of the small family-run firm.

However, a Stoy Hayward/London Business School survey* revealed that only 14% of small businesses actually survive into their third generation. Many problems occur within such organizations. Planning is often ill-disciplined. The culture of the business can be inflexible resulting in slow decision-making. Conflicts can arise where siblings of the founding father are rivals for control of the firm. In addition the competence of family members is often regarded to be of secondary importance to the need to offer employment. Professional managers, where employed, can feel stifled and frustrated. Objective business decisions are clouded by family sentiments. Sadly many family businesses go into decline when loyalties and emotional ties are placed above competence and performance.

1.4 SMALL BUSINESS CONCERNS

Growth is not always the panacea for success. Some companies will grow without any profit to show for it, and in some cases growth through over-trading may result in financial loss. Organizations faced with such a dilemma can easily face financial ruin. Where this happens, loss for the small business manager may even result in not only the business collapsing but other more personal deprivation being suffered beyond the confines of limited liability. Large businesses can afford temporary negative cash flow and losses which small businesses cannot. Cash flow can only be effectively managed by first establishing clear financial procedures and records.

Financial management will be a key performance indicator of the business and will also be a measure of the success of Total Quality once introduced. We will see later in this book that TQM will not only assist businesses to increase their market share but also to function on a financially sound basis through the elimination of waste, error and unnecessary effort. Furthermore the sound reputation gained from practising TQM will also favourably influence the

*Stoy Hayward/London Business School (1990) *Managing the Family Business in the UK, a report.*

6

decisions of potential investors so that when extra finance is required to support a business's expansion, investors will feel more confident in speculating with their money.

A second major concern of the small business person – lack of time – can be controlled by competent time management. Total Quality Management will enable staff to manage their time more effectively. It will aid the growth of the business through allowing the workforce, from the head of the organization to the lowest graded member of staff, to spend their allotted time at work on activities intended to improve the business. Time management alone will have a considerable effect on reducing waste – wasted time.

1.5 CHAPTER SUMMARY

- Many Western economies depend upon the success of the small business sector.
- The small business manager must demonstrate sufficient business acumen to be able to compete with larger organizations.
- National and local governments and state monopolies are now being fragmented and commercialized, many into small business entities, in order to expose their services to competition on the open market.
- Very small organizations are often single product companies and, as a result, need to look externally to detect changes in market trends and customer needs.
- Small businesses have the potential advantage of flexibility and speed of response over larger competitors.
- Successful small businesses go through a set pattern of growth from the inward-looking development of an idea and control of production or service provision to forward planning beyond immediate needs to take advantage of further growth opportunities.
- Many small businesses are family run. In such organizations there is a danger of placing family loyalties and emotions before objective decision-making.
- Time management and cash flow management are the primary concerns of many small business managers. TQM will help the control of cash by encouraging clear and effective financial

processes and encouraging investors to finance growth. Time management will enable the small business manager and his or her team to utilize their time more effectively for the benefit of the organization as a whole.

Quality – why bother? | 2

2.1 WHAT IS QUALITY?

There is little doubt, despite the wishes of some organizations ill prepared for change, that Total Quality has not only become firmly established but is here to stay. Its significance on world economies is equal to that of the industrial revolution of the last century. The customer is now becoming firmly established as reigning monarch of global economies.

In terms of definition, Quality can be stated as the satisfaction of agreed customer requirements. Total Quality can be defined as the mobilization of the whole organization to achieve Quality continuously and economically. These are the two themes that will pervade in this book. Many organizations have found to their peril that attempts to satisfy the ever-increasing demands of customers can result in increased expenditure, making for reduced profits or actual financial loss. TQM is a concept that will have the double benefit of not only satisfying the customer but also doing so in such a way that the organization gains significantly in its profitability. In other words, the external dimension of customer satisfaction will be mirrored by a capacity for internal cost savings achieved by a reduction in waste and inefficiency and a concentration on doing things right first time. It introduces the idea of internal customer satisfaction whereby each individual employee within the organization is a customer in his or her own right with needs and expectations to be met. In so doing, and as long as the process of 'conversion' of supplier inputs taking place within the organization to produce goods or services which the customer wants is sound, then the resultant effectiveness of the business will produce both delighted external customers and satisfied internal 'customer' staff and also drastically reduce operating costs. The often quoted results of TQM will be increased market share, flexibility of response to changing customer demands, a well-motivated workforce, higher output and greater profit. Non-profit-making organizations will also share the enormous benefits of better customer satisfaction, staff motivation and reduced costs. TQM is applicable to every field of activity, and as I will show towards the end of this book (Chapter 13) TQM will even pervade our social and domestic lives to affect communities and society at large.

Before examining quality definitions in detail, it is important not to construe quality, in our terms, as synonymous with 'prestige' or the preciousness associated with the quality of gem stones, for example. The well-worn analogy of the Rolls-Royce and the Ford Fiesta as both being 'quality' cars is worth reiterating to differentiate the terms. A Rolls-Royce is a motor car which meets a customer's requirement for transporting people from one point to another but in luxurious comfort and in such a way as to impress people on the way. A Ford Fiesta is no less a 'quality' car. Its purpose is to transport people from one location to another but in as cost-effective a manner as possible. Other factors such as reliability or safety, for example, are characteristics which apply to both and are shared requirements of their respective customers.

Quality 'gurus' – pioneers or specialists in the field of Total Quality – and the various quality standards which endorse quality management have all produced definitions of TQM. Most of these definitions are combinations of the two themes – customer satisfaction and economic cost – referred to above.

Some examples of Total Quality definitions together with their creators, all Quality luminaries in their own right, will illustrate the points made above:

- 'fitness for use or purpose' – Joseph Juran;
- 'conformance to requirements' – Philip Crosby;
- 'a predictable degree of uniformity and dependability at low cost and suited to the market' – W. Edwards Deming;
- ' . . . development, manufacture, administration and distribution of consistent low cost products and services that customers want and/or need' – Bill Conway.

10

An all embracing definition of Total Quality was produced by the British Quality Association in 1989. It will serve as a sufficient 'catch-all' description of concepts and techniques to be developed throughout this book:

Total Quality Management (TQM) is a corporate business management philosophy which recognizes that customer needs and business goals are inseparable. It is appropriate within both industry and commerce.

It ensures maximum effectiveness and efficiency within a business and secures commercial leadership by putting in place processes and systems which will promote excellence, prevent errors and ensure that every aspect of the business is aligned to customer needs and the advancement of business goals without duplication or waste of effort.

The commitment to TQM originates at the chief executive level in a business and is promoted in all human activities. The accomplishment of Quality is thus achieved by personal involvement and accountability, devoted to a continuous improvement process, with measurable levels of performance by all concerned.

It involves every department, function and process in a business and the active commitment of all employees to meeting customer need. In this regard the 'customers' of each employee are separately and individually identified.

2.2 HISTORICAL BACKGROUND

Modern-day TQM has its origins during the Second World War. The generally acknowledged founding father of TQM is W. Edwards Deming. An American statistician, he made a significant contribution to quality improvement in the United States through the use of statistical process control (SPC) – a subject discussed in greater depth in a later chapter of this book. He introduced American engineers in particular to the concept of SPC and pioneered scrap reductions and general quality improvements in materials for the American war effort. However, his reputation for quality improvement was established in post-war years when invited by General Douglas

McArthur to help the war-torn Japanese economy in its reconstruction efforts. His views on quality were accepted with enthusiasm in Japan, and he is credited by the Japanese as one of the primary causes of the so-called Japanese 'quality revolution'. The principle theme of his philosophy was the reduction of variability in product manufacture with the emphasis on statistical monitoring and control. If one compares Japanese goods of the 1950s and present-day Japanese goods, the difference in quality is largely due to Deming's influence.

Amongst Deming's more startling contentions was the assertion that only 6% of all quality problems were the result of worker incompetence, the remaining 94% were caused by poor management or inefficient business processes. Deming was a strong advocate of teamwork to resolve problems. He also criticized managers for running business on the basis of fear. By removing fear of blame or coercion from the workforce, he contended that employees could reach their full potential without the threat of rebuke when a mistake was made. His 14 points of action to establish and maintain Total Quality are regarded by many as the most succinct summary of Total Quality principles:*

1. Create consistency of purpose for improvement of production or service.
2. Adopt a new philosophy, i.e. no longer accept traditional delays, mistakes, etc.
3. Cease dependence on mass inspection.
4. End the practice of awarding business on the basis of the price tag.
5. Find problems and constantly improve the system of production and service.
6. Investigate modern methods of training on the job..
7. Instigate modern methods of supervision, less emphasis on numbers, i.e. quantity, and concentrate on quality.
8. Drive out fear from the organization.
9. Break down barriers between departments.
10. Eliminate numerical goals, posters and slogans for the workforce asking for new levels of productivity without providing methods.

*Edwards Deming, W. (1986) *Out of the Crisis*, Cambridge, Cambridge University Press.

11. Eliminate work standards that prescribe numerical quotas.
12. Remove the barriers to pride of workmanship.
13. Institute a vigorous programme of education and retraining.
14. Create a structure in top management which will allow everyone to work towards the transformation.

A second 'guru', Dr Joseph Juran, achieved equal fame in helping the Japanese instil Quality into their production facilities. His definition of quality – 'fitness for use or purpose' – is perhaps one of the most widely quoted definitions of all. Like Deming he advocated the reduction in process variability as the route to Quality improvement. He placed great emphasis on the need for good management and for the 'human element' of Quality to be developed, alleging that systems controlled by management caused at least 85% of the failures in any organization. He disliked slogan campaigns like 'right first time, every time' as sounding derogatory, making the point that people did not come to work to do a bad job, but by nature were concerned to do things right if allowed by management.

While these two thinkers were heavily influencing Japanese attitudes, back in the West, economies were taking a different course. In the economic growth of the post-war years, more and more emphasis was placed upon quantity rather than Quality. Conglomerates were formed. Bigger was better and goods of all description were mass produced in great volume. By the 1960s, however, Quality awareness was beginning to show. This decade was characterized by a growing consciousness of the consumer in the Quality of products. The reaction of manufacturers was to build in Quality inspection during the production process. This was the time when the Quality controller ruled supreme, with many organizations developing huge Quality control departments. The Quality of product did not improve, however, as individual employees made little personal improvement, seeing the responsibility for Quality as belonging somewhere else.

Significant change, however, occurred during the 1970s. The OPEC-induced oil crises resulted in a scarcity of energy resources and a general emphasis on Quality assurance to reduce waste. Energy saving campaigns abounded, speed restrictions were applied to transport and petrol was rationed or in short supply.

Meanwhile in Japan the Quality revolution was gathering pace. By the 1980s Western economies were shaken out of their complacency when traditional Western products (e.g. the camera and the motorbike) were suddenly overwhelmed by high Quality Japanese imports. The 1980s witnessed the apotheosis of Japanese economic achievement. Their pre-eminence resulted from a combination of technical excellence and uniform product Quality.

To remain in business the West was forced to reassess Quality. Ironically it took them some forty years before they could accept the doctrines of Juran and Deming as worthy of consideration. Nowadays most organizations in Western economies are coming to terms with Total Quality. More enlightened employers are also realizing that TQM represents not only market strategies and perfected systems but also a combination of technical know-how and the effective use of people. As one looks forward to the twenty-first century (Table 2.1), pundits predict that TQM will pervade every walk of life. Total Quality will not merely be a work-based practice but will dominate our communities and the very Quality of life itself. My own thoughts on this theme are expanded in Chapter 13.

Table 2.1 The history of Quality

1950s	–	Quantity not Quality.
1960s	–	Consumer awareness – inspection during the production process.
1970s	–	Scarcity of resources – Quality assurance to reduce waste.
1980s	–	Japanese pre-eminence in Quality through technical excellence.
1990s	–	Total Quality management – technical excellence and effective use of people.
2000	–	Quality of life and Quality in the community.

2.3 BS 5750/ISO 9000 AND TOTAL QUALITY

In Chapter 10 on Quality management systems I consider in depth the ubiquitous Quality management system BS 5750 and its international and European equivalents (ISO 9000 and EN 29000). At this juncture I will provide a few prefatory words on the subject as it is a potential source of confusion to many small business managers when contemplating TQM.

BS 5750, while intrinsically sound as an element of TQM, has attained great publicity from government-sponsored promotion, the plethora of BS 5750 consultants and the insistence of many large organizations for their suppliers to achieve registration to the standard in order to retain a continuing trading relationship. Public authorities in the United Kingdom, as an example of its pervasiveness, now normally require all potential suppliers and contractors to be registered before being eligible to tender for contracts. As a result many small businesses are caught in a dilemma – whether to prepare for BS 5750 registration or to embark on Total Quality. Many businesses have chosen the former route and some sadly consider that the sporting of the BS 5750 logo on their vehicles and letter-headed paper represents the achievement of TQM. This is not the case. BS 5750 should be an integral part of TQM rather than a stand-alone option. Its relationship to TQM – whilst important – is best placed in context by considering Fig. 2.1. TQM is where the three key elements of customer, staff and systems intersect.

If BS 5750 alone is progressed within an organization, undoubtedly benefits will ensue. However, the enormous advantages of Total Quality to be gained from heightened customer awareness and people development will be passed by or achieved belatedly when the

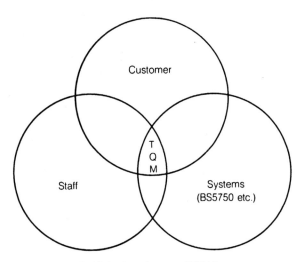

Figure 2.1 BS 5750/ISO 9000 in the context of TQM.

Table 2.2 Differences between BS 5750/ISO 9000 and TQM

BS 5750/ISO 9000	TQM
• Not necessarily customer focused	• Definitely customer focused
• Not integrated with corporate strategy	• Integral to company strategy
• Technical systems and procedures focused	• Philosophy concepts tools and techniques focused
• Employee involvement not necessary	• Emphasis on employee involvement and empowerment
• No focus on continuous improvement. BS5750/ISO 9000 – a decision	• Continuous improvement and TQM synonymous: TQM a never-ending journey
• Can be departmentally focused	• Organisation-wide – all departments, functions and levels
• Quality department responsible for quality	• Everyone responsible for quality
• More likely to preserve the status quo	• Involves process and culture change

organization realizes that even early registration to the standard will only give a temporary edge over the competition. Once all suppliers become registered firms, those who are also practising broader based Total Quality will remain in the ascendancy. John Pike and Richard Barnes in their book *TQM in Action** give an excellent comparison of the differences between BS 5750 and TQM as shown in Table 2.2.

In short BS 5750 will ensure that a business's Quality management system works – its paperwork is uniform, its product and services traceable, and procedures applied in the same manner throughout. BS 5750, however, will not emphasize customer orientation or continuous improvement. It is not organization wide and tends to preserve the status quo rather than cultivate a culture of change and flexibility. The often quoted three-step maxim of BS 5750 stated below indicates its value.

1. Document what you do.
2. Do only what you document.
3. Demonstrate that you have done it, by documentary proof.

This approach, alone, however, will not achieve Total Quality.

*Pike, J. and Barnes, R. (1994) *TQM in Action: A Practical Approach to Continuous Performance Improvement*, London, Chapman & Hall.

16

2.4 IMMEDIATE DECISIONS

A number of immediate decisions are required by the small business manager if his or her business is to be successful as a result of TQM. The title of this chapter 'Quality – why bother?' is perhaps the first question that should be addressed. In other words, 'what's in it for me?'. Answers to the question could be personal wealth, prestige and reputation, a more satisfying life, a fulfilled obligation to one's customers, one's staff and one's family, the survival of the business or the sheer pleasure of doing things right for a change. Whatever they may be, personal determination on the part of the small business manager is perhaps the key driving force to achieving Total Quality. The small business manager who is half-hearted or sceptical will almost certainly fail. If readers are interested but not convinced (which is only natural after having read a couple of chapters) perhaps the most immediate decision is to read this book through, then read other books on the subject, as well as periodicals, magazine articles, reports and so on. Attend local TQM seminars. Talk to colleagues in the local business community to attain their views on the subject. Only then, when fully convinced, take a decision either to adopt TQM whole heartedly or not to bother at all.

Having decided what to do, and assuming that the decision is to go ahead with TQM, the next decision is to plan – a subject dealt with in depth in the next chapter.

2.5 CHAPTER SUMMARY

- Total Quality Management is firmly established and likely to remain a permanent feature of business and commerce.
- Customer satisfaction at an economic cost are TQM's two distinguishing features.
- TQM is applicable to all types of business.
- Quality is concerned with meeting the requirements of the customer.

- TQM was first practised in Japan when introduced by Western management theorists to regenerate its post-war economy.
- Belatedly Western businesses have adopted TQM as the main business driver.
- BS 5750/ISO 9000 should not be confused with TQM. It should be viewed as an important part of Total Quality rather than Total Quality itself.
- Personal, customer, staff and company benefits are all potential advantages of TQM. The personal determination of the small business manager is the means of realizing these benefits.

PART TWO

Planning for
Total Quality

The planning process | 3

3.1 THE NEED FOR PLANNING

A prerequisite for establishing Total Quality is the need for careful
planning. All too often managers avoid this, preferring the excitement of activity to the inactivity of thought. The logical sequence
of Plan – Act – Review is very often contorted to Act – Review
–Correct – Plan. Total Quality becomes analogous to escaping a
minefield by feeling with one's feet, covering one's ears on the way
in case of unforseen explosions. Impatience to act has troubled
Western management to its cost. The demands of company
shareholders for early results has frequently led to companies taking
ill-considered decisions on introducing TQM with disastrous results.

The need for careful planning of the TQM process applies even
more so to the small business manager who, in many cases, lacks
the means to recover from wrongful decisions. One can imagine the
small business manager who has attended a one-day seminar on the
subject returning to the business bursting with enthusiasm to start
implementing immediately some of the typical 'Quality' activities
he or she was informed of. Such an approach will not work. Confusion will arise, initiatives will be uncoordinated, failures will ring
the death-knell for any improvement envisaged from TQM. As in
all activities, therefore, the planning stage is an essential forerunner
to action. The small business manager beset no doubt by a thousand
and one activities should not make the implementation of TQM one
thousand and two.

Continuing our scenario for the small business manager, let us
assume that through some source or other he or she has become

21

informed and enthused by Total Quality. The business may not be performing to expectation. Perhaps economic conditions, export tariffs or the loss of a significant market to overseas competition is having a damaging effect on business performance. Poor product quality, low staff morale or high materials wastage may be issues of great concern. The fêted benefits of low operational costs and satisfied customers would entice any entrepreneur in such circumstances to take TQM seriously. The small business manager has personally become informed and committed to the concept of Total Quality. But none of the manager's colleagues have yet. For the manager now to rush the introduction of a number of TQM activities like a cost of quality analysis, a customer survey or the introduction of statistical process controls would well-nigh annihilate any hopes there might have been for TQM to improve the business. The first step must be to plan. And in that planning process, senior colleagues must also become involved informed and committed to the idea of TQM.

Case study: The benefits of planning

A well-known industrial conglomerate decided to construct two identical chemical plants at sites in the United Kingdom and Japan respectively. Each project was under the control of a local management team. An examination of the activities of the British team revealed that within three months of commencement the British plant was well under construction. Within six months it was virtually complete, by which time the Japanese had barely cut the first sod of turf to lay foundations.

The British construction team ploughed ahead completing the plant well ahead of schedule, while the Japanese were still way behind. However, before the British plant came into full production, problems began to emerge. These were dismissed initialy as mere 'teething troubles'. Nevertheless such problems continued to such a degree that major replanning and reconstruction was necessary to make the plant operational.

Meanwhile in Japan, after inordinate planning, construction commenced. The project progressed flawlessly. Every possible pitfall had been considered and planned for. By the outcome the Japanese had completed their project on schedule and to plan. Through careful planning the Japanese plant became fully operational ahead of its British counterpart by a significant margin.

3.2 COMMENCING THE PLANNING PROCESS

Perhaps the best way of commencing the planning process would be for the small business manager with the team of senior staff to convene a meeting off-site – and thereby free from interruption – to examine the business in its entirety. Such a meeting could be chaired by the small business manager personally or the services of an external management consultant could be employed. The latter option would allow the manager to play a more impartial role, inhibiting his or her colleagues less from making critical observations of the way the business is currently run. An added benefit of meeting off-site would be to encourage more junior staff remaining on-site to take responsibility for the running the business in the absence of the management team. (The idea of empowering staff to take greater control and responsibility for their own jobs and the success of the company will be developed in later chapters.) The purpose of such a meeting could be to highlight the strengths and weaknesses of the business and consider whether some immediate remedial action is appropriate or not, or in fact whether further analysis of the business is necessary to obtain a clearer picture. Juxtaposed to this diagnosis, the small business manager would do well to set out the relatively straightforward principles of Total Quality. Such principles would include the following:

- Everyone in the organization understands the customer's requirements and how the company is performing to achieve those requirements.
- Everyone's role is clear and everyone understands how their own role and that of their section or department contributes to the satisfaction of customer requirements.
- Everyone within the organization is both a customer and supplier of someone else and should strive continuously to satisfy customers both internally and externally.

23

- Measures of business performance are agreed upon and understood.
- The senior management of the organization is acting in unison to give a clear direction for the business which concentrates effort on the key measures of performance.

A useful beginning to such a 'workshop' would be to conduct an analysis of the strengths, weaknesses, opportunities and threats (SWOT analysis) of the business. In conducting such an analysis the small business manager (or consultant) would elicit and record the strengths and weaknesses of the business and the opportunities and threats emerging. The following case study shows the results of an actual SWOT analysis for a small light engineering company.

Case study: SWOT analysis

Below is an example of an actual SWOT analysis from a small light engineering company:

Strengths:
- Staff
- Reputation
- Diverse technology
- BS 5750 registration
- Profitability

- Sound balance sheet
- Operating in International markets

Opportunities:
- Cost Reduction
- Capital investment
- Expansion
- New markets
- Increased manufacturing volume
- Acquisitions

Weaknesses:
- Site limitations

- Excess capacity

- Work in progress
- Job role clarification
- Aging machinery
- Limited product range
- Foreign language skills

Threats:
- Far Eastern competition
- Exchange rate fluctuations
- Product obsolescence
- Risk of takeover
- Foreign legislation
- Export/import tariffs

Following the SWOT analysis three basic questions need to be posed at a planning workshop, namely the following:

- Where are we now?
- Where do we want to be?
- How do we get there?

Answers to these three questions are fundamental in implementing any process of improvement. Some suggested subject areas to consider in answering these questions are contained within Figure 3.1.

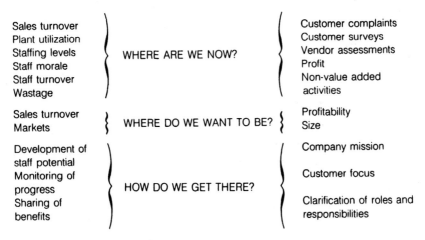

Figure 3.1 The Quality improvement model.

A general corporate analysis could be undertaken using the checklist contained in Table 3.2. Perhaps a categorization of the products or services produced by the small business manager would be a useful exercise to focus collectively on which products or services are likely to generate profits. Figure 3.2 would be an effective way of undertaking such a categorization, whereby each product or service is coded according to the standard business planning terminology of 'cash cows', 'dogs', 'rising stars' and 'owner's egos'.

25

Table 3.2 An example of a corporate analysis

Output	–	Rising/falling
Scrap/waste	–	Rising/falling
Time to perform tasks	–	Increasing/decreasing
Time to learn how to perform tasks	–	Increasing/decreasing
Machine and equipment utilization	–	Rising/falling
Accidents	–	Rising/falling
Staff turnover	–	Rising/falling
Absenteeism	–	Rising/falling
Delays	–	Increasing/decreasing
Disputes	–	Increasing/decreasing
Customer complaints	–	Increasing/decreasing

The planning workshop should consider each of these issues in full. The duration of such meetings often extends over a period of two to three days dependent on the complexity of matters emerging. Although in many instances it may not be practicable for the small business manager and his immediate team to spend such a length of time away from the business, it is essential that fundamental concerns which do arise are considered in detail.

The outputs from such a workshop could include:

- a basic understanding of TQM gained by the whole management team;
- an agreed company mission statement;
- allocation of roles and responsibilities for each member of the management team in implementing TQM;
- a series of management actions by both the team as a whole and each individual team member;
- a TQM plan of implementation together with an agreed communication and involvement strategy for the remainder of the workforce;
- dates for a series of review meetings to assess progress.

Whereas many of the issues likely to emerge from the initial planning workshop will be dealt with in depth in subsequent chapters of this book, company mission statements and the allocation of roles and responsibilities are points worth considering now.

26

Product/service	Cash cow	Dog	Rising star	Owner's ego

Definition: Cash cows: good profit for very little effort
          Dogs: money losers
          Rising stars: tomorrow's cash cows
          Owner's ego: tomorrow's dogs

Figure 3.2 Product/service categorization.

27

3.3 DEVELOPING A MISSION STATEMENT

One of the essentials of the planning process is the formation of a mission statement. A mission statement is a pattern of words which encapsulates a vision of the success and future direction of an organization. In many organizations the mission statement represents the vision of the chief executive alone, which by force of personality or strength of leadership, he or she has convinced the management team to adopt as the way forward. There is no guarantee, however, that all of the managers will be fully committed to the mission, let alone the remainder of the workforce. Ideally, therefore, the preparation of this statement should involve as many employees as possible. In this way there will be a greater chance, because of the involvement of staff, of everyone being committed to its fulfilment. In larger organizations this may not be a practical option. The small business manager, however, does have the advantage of size in obtaining the thoughts of others before preparing a mission statement.

I have already advocated in this chapter that a mission statement be one of the products of an off-site TQM planning workshop. It would be no mean feat, however, if managers attending the workshop were to solicit the views of their staff beforehand so that what is produced does have the shared ownership of the workforce at large. Many employees at the outset of TQM may be unfamiliar with the concept of a mission statement and feel uneasy about making any contribution. An alternative approach – especially if communications mechanisms are sound – would be for each manager at the planning workshop to agree a draft statement which could be ratified or amended at specially convened departmental meetings. Proposed amendments or alternative points of view could then be considered at a subsequent management workshop.

The development of a mission statement in this way is an example of a theme I will constantly propound throughout this handbook, namely that the involvement of staff in the process of continuous improvement is one of the basic insignia of Total Quality.

In developing a mission statement, there are a number of early considerations which should be taken into account. First the statement should not be too long. Two to three paragraphs at most would

28

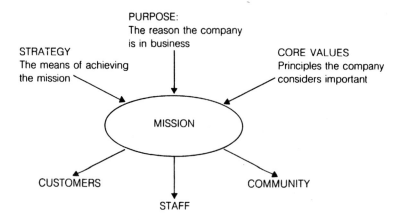

Figure 3.3 Elements of a mission statement.

suffice. Matters to consider informing the statement could include business strategy, core values (i.e. what the company holds most dear), business purpose, standards and behaviour. Many organizations in the preparation of a business mission also include reference to the customer, staff and sometimes the local community. The ingredients of a mission statement are portrayed in Figure 3.3.

The mission statement should be easy to read, short enough to hold an individual's attention and sufficiently upbeat to act as a source of motivation within the organization and as a source of reassurance without.

Even very large organizations produce mission statements of elegance in the brevity and simplicity of their message. This is demonstrated in this example from a large high street banking organization:

> The mission of the Company is to be the UK's leading financial retailer through understanding and meeting our customer needs and by being more professional and innovative than our competitors.

The following case study illustrates the stages involved in preparing a mission statement and immediate management actions thereafter.

Case study: The creation of a mission

A small manufacturing organization grappling with the issues of Total Quality following a recent management buyout organized a TQM planning workshop under the chairmanship of the newly appointed managing director. The management team present approached the workshop in the following way.

- Each manager produced a list of significant words, following consultation with their own departmental staff, to be included in the make-up of the mission statement. Words were allocated to three categories, namely customers, staff and community.
- A three-paragraph statement was then drafted – and subsequently ratified by the workforce – equating to each of the three categories.
- To achieve the mission, a list of actions was agreed upon which the management team had to undertake.
- To avoid confusion of role and responsibility, general management actions were broken down into individual management activities with a time period for completion set against each action point.

A further workshop was convened three months later to review all the actions agreed.

Once finalized the mission statement should be given high visibility. It should be displayed in the company's reception area and on the desk of the small business manger. The statement should be on display to the whole workforce whether they are situated at one or a number of locations and should be amended by consensus from time to time to take account of any developing trends within the business.

Some examples of actual mission statements are given below.

- A leisure organization providing educational and recreational residential courses to young people:

The Company will create an environment which offers opportunity for children and adults to enjoy educational and social activities in a safe, residential context. Similarly, experiences and activities will be provided in a professional manner which will underpin the intentions of the Company and fulfil the values of the parent movement.

- A family-owned engineering company in the locomotive industry:

The Company is a worldwide leader in steam locomotive products and services. Our mission is to improve continually our products and services, innovating where necessary, to satisfy and delight our customers. In this way we will be able to expand and prosper as a business.

There are three basic values which underpin our Company mission. These are:

- Our staff – our staff are the source of our strength. Their skills ensure the quality of our reputation and product. Staff involvement and teamwork are one of our core human values.
- Our products – our products are the end result of our efforts, and they should be the best in serving customers worldwide. We are judged by the quality of our products.
- Our profits – profits are the ultimate measure of how effectively we meet our customers' requirements. We must make profits to survive and prosper.

- A horticultural nursery:

The Company is dedicated to producing products and services that meet the requirements of its customers at all times.

It is the Company's intention to maintain its leading position in the market through the provision of superior customer satisfaction levels.

All employees must have a positive commitment to quality and respond quickly and effectively to achieve the performance standards set.

Each employee is a customer for work done by other employees or suppliers, with a right to expect good work from others to contribute to the corporate goal of customer satisfaction.

In larger businesses or companies with many locations a local site mission may have a more immediate impact. A local mission should support the company-wide mission.

If the size of the business permits, the small business manager should also encourage departmental mission statements. These will allow each department to recognize its role and contribution to the overall mission of the business. However, this will not be necessary in very small organizations as there should not be any difficulty in each department or section identifying with the company mission. An example of a personnel department mission in the financial service industry illustrates the value of departmental mission statements:

> We shall provide defect-free products and services to our internal and external customers which meet their agreed needs. We shall do so on time, first time and every time. Only by doing this will we achieve our mission to be the UK's leading financial retailer.

As with company-wide mission statements, departmental missions should, wherever possible, result from the input of all staff. This will encourage a sense of staff involvement and ownership of the repsonsibility for achieving the misison.

3.4 EDUCATION, POLICY AND RESPONSIBILITY

An overriding factor, in addition to the mission statement, is the commitment of the small business manager and his or her immediate team of managers to the concept of Quality. It is important to establish this at the very beginning of a TQM initiative. Without an almost obsessional belief in TQM as not only the way forward but also the salvation of the organization, it will be difficult to achieve any meaningful commitment throughout the rest of the company. In very small organizations, obviously the overt commitment of the small business manager will become readily apparent. However, in companies employing in excess of, say, a hundred staff there will be a far greater need for the small business manager to rely on the commitment and enthusiasm of his or her managers. Understanding is an intrinsic element of commitment. In addition to personal commitment, the small business manager should encourage all of his managers to gain a wider understanding of the subject by attending external seminars on TQM. Subscriptions to specialist TQM magazines and a wide reading of the many specialist books on the subject are equally important in increasing one's understanding of the subject. Issues of communicating and training will become early priorities. The engagement of an external Total Quality trainer or, better still, in-house training of the workforce conducted by the small business manager and his or her team of immediate managers are the usual routes to widening an understanding of TQM within the organization. Certainly if awareness training of this nature is undertaken tier by tier with the ranks of junior managers or supervisors educating their immediate teams of staff, then an unequivocal message will be sent forth that the company is totally committed to TQM.

In support of the mission statement is the need for a quality policy. The quality policy expounds upon the principles contained within the mission. It will foster a shift of emphasis from the control and inspection of a product or service to error prevention. The policy will also serve to heighten sensitivity to customer requirements and introduce the idea of a shared responsibility for providing a first-class product or service.

Some of the basic elements of a quality policy are contained in Figure 3.4. Each principle is dealt with in depth at relevant points throughout this book.

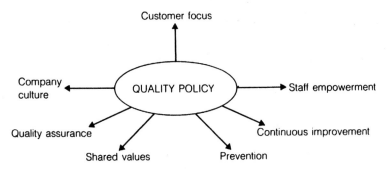

Figure 3.4 Basic elements of a Quality policy.

To illustrate a quality policy, I have drafted a composite document drawn from a number of small company quality policies as follows.

Quality policy

1. Quality is the responsiblity of the whole workforce.
2. The management team will instil a culture which empowers all staff to assume this responsibility.
3. The emphasis for quality improvement will be placed on each and every individual within the organization.
4. Responsibility for failure will be collective as will the responsibility for success. Success or failure will therefore be shared by all.
5. An enabling culture will be established based upon the belief that people are essentially responsible and will do a good job.
6. The role of the management team should be to create the conditions for this to happen.

Turning to the division of responsibilities within the management team, all too often when assisting small businesses one of the early pitfalls I have discovered is a lack of clarity as to which member of the team is responsible for what when it comes to implementing Total Quality. Small business managers and departmental heads will undertake a multitude of roles and responsibilties which inevitably leads to confusion and overlap. Before even turning to the individual repsonsibilities for implementing TQM it would behove the small business manager well to clarify or restate the job responsibilities of each individual manager. Having done so the next task will be to allocate particular areas of responsibility for TQM to individual team members. In doing this, some companies use the term 'champion'. In other words each manager will champion a particular aspect of TQM and will be accountable for its successful implementation. Areas of responsibility typically allocated to management team members will include:

- communications
- quality assurance systems (BS 5750/ISO 9000)

- supplier relationships
- business process analysis
- cost of quality
- staff training
- customer surveys.

Some of the responsibilities will have natural champions. Cost of Quality could very well become the responsibility of the finance manager, customer surveys the responsibility of the marketing manager. Other responsibilities will be more difficult to allocate. The small business manager would be well advised to allocate some of the more intricate or enjoyable responsibilities to members of the team who are suspected of not perhaps being one hundred per cent committed to TQM. Accountability and pressure to conform from fellow managers will act as a powerful stimulus for them to develop a commitment to TQM.

The small business management team should act as a Quality Steering Group or Quality Implementation Team adopting a coordinating role for the whole TQM initiative. The role of this team is described in greater detail in Chapter 8 when addressing teamwork.

3.5 THE QUALITY MANAGER

An important role in the implementation of TQM is that of the Quality manager. Many organizations make the mistake of designating this role as one of Quality control, inspecting products or services during the process of production, or worse still of being responsible for the whole TQM process. The former role, whereby the Quality manager acts as Quality controller, will merely confirm the traditional perception of Quality as a checking activity after the event. It will allow employees to escape personal responsiblitity for their own Quality, as they will know full well that if poor Quality is produced it will be the responsibility of someone else to detect it. Companies which offload TQM in its entirety onto the Quality manager are also liable to failure. In such a role the Quality manager will act as a convenient scapegoat when TQM fails, when the real reason for failure will be a lack of commitment coming from the top of the company.

In essence the role of the Quality manager is one of coordination. He or she should report directly to the small business manager and have the prime responsibility of coordinating all the activities of the TQM process. Large organizations engaged in TQM frequently appoint a full-time Quality manager. This may be a luxury which the small business manager can ill afford. In small organizations therefore the role is often combined with other functions and responsibilities. I have seen the role successfully fulfilled by company secretaries, training managers, PAs to the managing director or former Quality control managers. In addition to coordinating the overall TQM process Quality managers often coordinate the process of achieving BS 5750 registration.

In selecting a Quality manager the small business manager should first decide whether he or she has sufficient staff resources to make the appointment an exclusive full-time job. Once this has been decided, an individual should be selected with good organizational skills and the ability to influence and persuade. Very often the Quality manager will be cast in the role of change agent and will have to be skilful in inducing others to adopt a fundamental change of attitude or work practice without always having to call upon the small business manager to force change through in person. If the management team were to designate themselves as the Quality Implementation Team, then the Quality manager would be responsible for presenting regular TQM progress reports at team meetings. He or she would also act as a point of liaison with any external consultancy assistance utilized, government agencies or quality assurance (BS 5750/ISO 9000) registration bodies.

The Quality manager should ideally already possess an extensive knowledge of TQM, or if not should receive thorough training in every aspect of the subject. He or she should act as 'resident expert' advising the small business manager and the rest of the workforce on the finer points of the implementation process.

An example of an actual job description of a Quality manager within a small business is given in Figure 3.5. One can see how the job description carefully emphasizes the advisory and coordination roles of the function.

Job title:	Quality Manager Job holder:
Responsible to:	Managing Director
Responsible for:	One administrator/typist (part time)
Job purpose:	To coordinate every activity related to the Company's Total Quality Management process and to advise the Managing Director and his board of managers of quality-related matters on a regular basis.

Duties and responsibilities:

1. To act as a contact point both internally and externally on TQM issues.

2. To coordinate the staff Quality awareness, communications and training programmes, liaising as necessary with the respective management Quality 'champions'.

3. To report on a regular basis to the Quality Steering Group and on a day-to-day basis to the Managing Director on TQM implementation progress.

4. To advise the Quality Steering Group and Managing Director where necessary on appropriate sources of external consultancy and training assistance relating to TQM.

5. To undertake specific staff training and development activities in Quality related matters.

6. To coordinate the BS 5750 registration project, including the activities of the Company's internal quality auditors and external liaison with the appointed BS 5750 registration body.

7. To facilitate where necessary corrective action and quality improvement teams.

8. To assist all production and administrative staff to improve all aspects of their operations through the adoption of TQM.

Figure 3.5 A Quality manager's job description.

3.6 ORGANIZATION DESIGN

An important consideration in the planning of TQM is company structure. When implementing TQM, an organization should be viewed as a processor of goods or services (inputs) received from external suppliers to meet specific customer requirements (outputs). Resources are brought to bear in the form of people, machinery or materials. Controls are applied in the form of procedures and regulations as shown in Figure 3.6.

However, it is the manner in which goods or services are processed within an organization that will make the difference between good and bad Quality outputs. Many large organizations are very hierarchical in structure with tightly defined responsibilities. There is a tendency in such companies for staff to show allegiance to their department rather than to the organization as a whole. Departments become insular, and inter-departmental squabbles frequently flare up as departmental managers defend their territory. Such a vertical structure conflicts with the process of manufacture or service provision which flows laterally across companies as inputs are converted to outputs. In addition to friction between departments the contradiction between process and structure will lead to a blame culture in which departments are cast as scapegoats by others when Quality suffers and customers are disappointed. The irony of this is that many problems which do emerge are not necessarily the fault of one particular department, but occur at the interface of departments where suspicion, lack of understanding and conflicting loyalties abound. Where there is a lack of company-wide teamwork

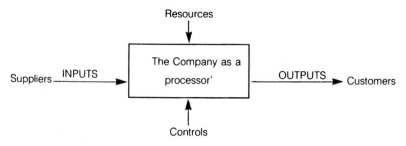

Figure 3.6 The 'processor' view of the organization.

even the most mundane issues will be dealt with at the highest levels within the company. It is only at this point that individuals have responsibilities which traverse the departments in dispute. Figure 3.7 illustrates the conflict between process flow and hierarchical structure.

As developed in Chapter 6 a better way to view the organization would be as a series of interlocking teams running horizontally across the organization to match the flow of business processes. As a result of a team-based view of the organization, many companies have removed whole tiers of middle management in an effort to create a matrix structure where multi-disciplinary teams are formed to address particular processes and to develop a more acute customer orientation.

Fortunately in a small business context, vast hierarchies are not normally in evidence. Nevertheless, the small business manager should be aware of the rivalries and conflicts that can arise in a rigidly structured organization. In planning a team-based approach to TQM, the small business manager would do well to consider flattening the organizational structure and redefine resultant roles and responsibilities, perhaps allocating superfluous supervisory staff to functions emerging during the process of TQM implementation.

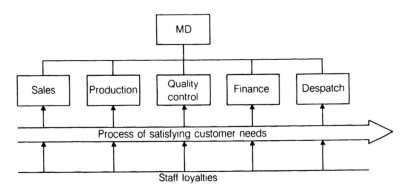

Figure 3.7 The 'traditional' view of the organization.

3.7 CHAPTER SUMMARY

- Planning is an essential prerequisite to the implementation of Total Quality.
- At the outset of the planning process the small business manager should ensure the involvement and commitment of his or her immediate team of managers.
- An off-site planning 'workshop' of the management team is a useful start to the planning process.
- Roles and responsibilities of the management team as a whole and each individual team member should be clearly defined.
- The management team should create and communicate a mission statement stipulating the future direction of the organization together with its core values. Input from the remainder of the workforce in this process will be an additional benefit.
- The management team should become familiar with the concepts of TQM by means of in-house and external training and education.
- A quality policy should be created to expand upon the principles contained within the mission statement.
- Wherever possible the post of Quality manager should be created to coordinate the activities of TQM.
- A team-based approach to Quality should be adopted which avoids hierarchical or departmentalized company structures.

Quality diagnosis

4.1 QUALITY REVIEW

As we have seen in the preceding chapter, a primary step in implementing Total Quality is to establish where the organization stands in terms of current quality. Only then, having secured a base point, can improvements commence. The so called diagnostic stage of TQM is of considerable importance to the small business manager. Essentially there are six diagnostic steps to take in establishing the current state of quality, namely:

- the opinion of customers
- the opinion of employees
- business processes currently in use
- the cost of quality
- a review of suppliers
- benchmarking of performance.

These stages and their impact on TQM are portrayed in Figure 4.1. The first three stages listed I will deal with in this chapter. The remainder are covered in separate chapters in their own right.

It is important for the small business manager not to ignore the process of diagnosis. Some organizations do, assuming that they already know this information, and act on the basis of false premises often leading to disastrous results.

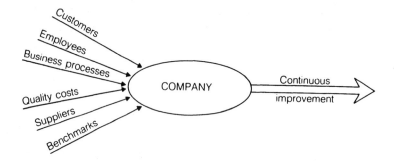

Figure 4.1 The diagnosis of Quality.

4.2 CUSTOMER REVIEW

We have seen already that the essence of TQM is satisfying customer requirements. The obvious way of doing this is to ask them. It is surprising to note, however, how many organizations do not ask their customers such basic questions as the following.

- Are we meeting your requirements as customer?
- What problems are you experiencing?
- How can we help resolve your problems?
- How do we, as an organization, compare to our competitors?

Many organizations assume that they know what their customers feel either through misplaced arrogance or from haphazard information gained from informal contacts alone. Many consider that they are satisfying customer requirements through the absence of formal customer complaints. Often these assumptions are wrong. Actions based on wrongful conjecture of customer requirements can force companies out of business. This threat looms large no less for the small business. Whereas large organizations may have a sufficient customer base, resources or market share to overcome the loss of some customers, the small business is particularly exposed. For many small organizations the loss of a major customer could make the difference between survival and failure.

To obtain the views of customers, some form of questionnaire should be devised which is either presented in writing to the customer or through face-to-face interview. Before examining the nature of information to be obtained let us review the various options available to the small business manager. If the small business operates in a retailing context and is visited by its customers (shops, garages, doctors or solicitors' practices) then actual questionnaire documentation can be placed on site for customers to complete either while on the premises or to be returned on the next visit or by post. In the case of an organization undertaking inter-company trading either a postal or telephone questionnaire would be the more appropriate approach.

In undertaking a customer survey, first prepare a list of current customers. Depending upon numbers the small business manager could either survey all of his customers or take a representative (say 10%) sample poll. Either method should produce information of value on current performances. The design of the questionnaire should incorporate a number of basic questions as follows.

- What are your requirements of me as a supplier organization?
- What particular aspects of my service to you as a cusotmer do I do well?
- What particular aspects do I do badly?
- Where can I improve my performance?
- What new products or services would you be interested in which I could possibly supply?

It is important to avoid excessively long questionnaires, whether these are to be completed by customers on site, or to be returned by post. It is also important to be specific in the question format. Bland general questions will not reproduce enough hard-hitting information for the small business manager to act upon.

An example of a customer survey is given in Figure 4.2. It is an extract from the questionnaire provided by a small garden centre which had decided to survey its customers on the shop floor.

Survey questionnaires obviously should also have an accompanying letter of explanation together with, in the case of postal surveys, a stamped addressed envelope for convenience of return.

CUSTOMER SURVEY - SPECIMEN

1. Approximately how often do you visit this garden centre each year?

   March-September ....

   October-February ....

   Total visits each year ....

2. What type of goods do you tend to buy from this garden centre? (Please tick as appropriate).

Outdoor plants & shrubs	☐	Pets	☐
House plants	☐	Garden furniture	☐
Garden tools	☐	Paving/fencing	☐
Plant pots/accessories	☐	Shed/summerhouse	☐
Plant feed/soil/fertilizer	☐	Greenhouse conservatory	☐

   Other (please specify) ....

3. What is your overall impression of this garden centre?

   ....

   ....

   ....

   ....

4. In your opinion, what are its main strengths and weaknesses?

   Strengths ....

   ....

   Weaknesses ....

   ....

44

5. How would you rate different aspects of our service? Please provide a score for each of the following on a scale of 1 to 10 where 1 is very poor and 10 is excellent.

Quality of plants	....	Helpful staff	....
Variety of plants	....	Knowledgeable staff	....
How plants are displayed	....	Staff appearance	....
Price tags/labels	....	Parking facilities	....
Value for money	....	Opening hours	....
Layout of garden centre	....	Delivery service	....
Cleanliness/tidiness	....	Range of goods on offer	....

Overall rating of this garden centre ....

6. Overall, do you feel that our level of service to the customer has declined, improved or stayed the same over the past 3 years?

Improved ☐

Stayed the same ☐

Declined ☐

Don't know ☐

7. What improvements or new services would you like to see introduced in the future?

....

....

....

....

Figure 4.2 An extract from a customer survey.

CUSTOMER SURVEY

**HELP US TO GIVE YOU AN EVEN BETTER SERVICE – AND
COLLECT YOUR FREE GIFT VOUCHER WORTH £5.00.**

As an organization we are committed to customer care and are continually
reviewing our standards of quality and service.

This survey has been designed to collect information on how satisfied you
are with our current level of service and the goods we have on offer, as
well as establishing the type of improvements you would like us to introduce
in the future.

Your cooperation in this survey will help us give you an even better service
in the future. But as a token of our thanks, please accept a FREE gift voucher
worth £5.00 when you hand your completed questionnaire to any member
of our staff.

Figure 4.3 An example of a letter accompanying a customer survey questionnaire.

For example, the actual letter accompanied the retail questionnaire,
a sample of which was given in Figure 4.2, is shown in Figure 4.3.
Note the inducement of a free gift to encourage customers to complete the document.

Telephone questionnaires also need specific information. A
previously prepared written script will help considerably in keep-
ing the conversation to the point. If possible avoid becoming involved
in lengthy discussions on particular customer responses. The hiring
of market researcher to act on behalf of the company may be a
wise option in order to preserve objectivity in the conduct of
the survey.

The results of survey data received should be analysed and
categorized by customer type. A list of priority improvement actions
will emerge which can be the subject of consideration at the next
scheduled meeting of the management team.

4.3 STAFF OPINIONS

A second important source of information about a company's performance may be obtained from staff themselves. Two methods are usually adopted. One is through informal group discussions, the second method is via formal questionnaires. It is for the small business manager to decide which is the most appropriate method. The size of the organization may well determine which choice to make. Group discussions in a small organization have the benefit of informality and can encourage free comment on current issues. An anonymous questionnaire would allow comments that people coul' feel uncomfortable to state in open discussion. However, in a very small business, staff may be reluctant to be overtly critical for fear of being recognized via their handwriting, despite the anonymity of the questionnaire. A similar problem undermines the use of informal group discussion. Staff may well feel very nervous of criticizing their employer to his face and will almost certainly not raise any personal criticisms of managers who may be present regarding their own behaviour or performance. The same inhibitions will arise in the case of criticizing work colleagues. The result of such an exercise, if conducted 'in house', could be a mild series of generalities which would not give enough hard information, especially about management attitudes and behaviour, to enable the small business manager to take any specific action.

A way of avoiding such a problem for group opinion surveys would be to engage an outside consultant to conduct an impartial opinion survey. The consultant could work to a set script and stress that the purpose of the survey is to obtain honest opinion without any personal redress to individuals commenting. Handwriting recognition in anonymous questionnaires could be overcome by constructing a questionnaire in such a way as to confine comment to 'box ticking' according to the degree of agreement with prerecorded statements. Fear of identification will prove a strong indicator of the current culture that pervades the business. If such is the case, the small business manager will have to take action to change attitudes if the company is to adopt the spirit of openness and cooperation which typifies Total Quality organizations.

In designing a staff opinion survey, some of the topics to be covered should include:

- TQM awareness
- customer awareness
- manager/staff relations
- teamwork
- communications
- job satisfaction
- staff training.

It is worthwhile also not to group questions by subject area but to mix them in random fashion so that staff are not lulled into giving set responses to each topic.

Case Study: Staff opinion survey by group discussion

A college of technology with over 1000 students and some 80 staff, during the process of implementing Total Quality, engaged a management consultant to undertake an opinion survey to assess the success of the TQM initiative to date.

The method adopted was for the college principal to write a general memorandum to all staff, which was also displayed on notice boards and discussed at departmental staff meetings. The document explained the purpose of the survey and the need for constant feedback on the progress of TQM.

To commence the process, the consultant conducted one-to-one confidential interviews with each member of the college management team, using a structured questionnaire to ensure consistency of subject matter under discussion. Similar discussions were then held with groups of staff, selected at random from all areas of the college. The same questionnaire format was used in group discussions as in the management interviews.

Common themes were extracted from the interviews and group discussions and presented back to the college's management team in report format.

The response of the management team (recorded after a few days' contemplation) was added to the report and re-presented to the same groups of staff originally interviewed. The report was also distributed to the remainder of staff via a special staff bulletin. It was discussed in depth during a series of staff briefing sessions, all of which the principal chaired in person.

The essence of successful opinion surveys is communicating to staff the rationale of the exercise beforehand, the giving of feedback after the event, and most importantly, **acting** upon the results. In the case study quoted above the feedback process was considered a very important aspect of the whole exercise. It showed the openness of the college management in taking account of the opinions of staff when implementing change.

Two examples of written questionnaires are given in Figures 4.4 and 4.5. Figure 4.4, which is an extract from a service organization staff survey, is designed to encourage free comment; Figure 4.5, taken from a small manufacturing company, is more restrictive in its responses through the use of a 'tick box' method of completion.

Some final points on staff opinion surveys would include the attachment of an introductory letter to the survey from the small business manager in person stating the purpose of the survey and what will happen thereafter. The survey could be construed as a mechanism to gain the views of staff on the key issues concerning the implementation of TQM and to identify how staff feel about the organization and its effect on their ability to provide a Quality product or service. It is also worth the small business manager stressing that there will be no recriminations on individuals as a result of what they have written or said and that the purpose of the exercise is to gain honest opinion on the current state of the company.

4.4 BUSINESS PROCESS ANALYSIS

In addition to asking one's staff and customers to comment on the condition of the company and to make suggestions for improvement, a very important means of determining current performance is to analyse all current processes which occur within the business. We

Staff Opinion Survey

Circle the appropriate response and comment where appropriate in the space provided.

	Strongly Disagree	Disagree	Agree	Strongly Agree
1. I have been made aware of and understand the Company's Mission and business targets.	1	2	3	4
Comment:				
2. My manager and I communicate well.	1	2	3	4
Comment:				
3. I am given enough authority to do my job effectively.	1	2	3	4
Comment:				
4. My working environment promotes a high level of performance.	1	2	3	4
Comment:				
5. There is a high level of quality awareness within the Company at all levels.	1	2	3	4
Comment:				

	Strongly Disagree	Disagree	Agree	Strongly Agree
6. The Company gives good customer service.	1	2	3	4
Comment:				
....				
....				
7. I am allowed sufficient time to provide a quality service.	1	2	3	4
Comment:				
....				
....				
8. I feel a real sense of pride in being part of the Company.	1	2	3	4
Comment:				
....				
....				
9. My manager provides vision and inspires commitment to quality and productivity by setting high standards.	1	2	3	4
Comment:				
....				
....				
10. I work as part of a team and am allowed to exchange freely ideas and opinions with my colleagues.	1	2	3	4
Comment:				
....				
....				
11. I am kept well informed about decisions that affect me.	1	2	3	4
Comment:				
....				
....				

Figure 4.4 Extract from a service organization staff opinion survey.

Staff Survey Questionnaire

Please indicate the degree to which you agree with the following statements by ticking the appropriate box.

Key: 1. Not at all
2. Slightly
3. Moderately
4. Mostly
5. Completely

		1	2	3	4	5
1.	I feel a sense of pride in being part of the Company.					
2.	There is a high level of Quality awareness in the Company.					
3.	The Company provides good Quality products.					
4.	The Company gives good customer service					
5.	The Company gives good value for money.					
6.	The Company's management provides effective leadership.					
7.	I work in a group which has a great deal of team spirit.					
8.	I am kept well informed about decisions that affect me.					
9.	I understand the requirement for the work that I provide to others.					
10.	Our most important priority is meeting the customers' needs and expectations.					
11.	The product and information supplied supplied to me (from within my own work group, or from other work groups) is always:					
	(a) correct					
	(b) on time.					
12.	I understand how my work group contributes to the Company's aims.					
13.	I am allowed to take action to improve Quality.					
14.	I would like to make an additional contribution to the improvement of Quality.					

Figure 4.5 Extract from a manufacturing organization staff survey questionnaire.

have already seen in Fig. 3.6 that a company should be viewed as a converter of inputs from suppliers to outputs for customers. We will also see in Chapter 6 that in order to satisfy external customers each individual within the organization should be viewed as both an internal customer and an internal supplier. Before developing these concepts the third area of diagnosis should be an examination of what actually goes on inside the business in the course of process conversion.

We can define a process as follows:

A sequence of activities which produces an output or result from the transformation of inputs through the controlled application of resources.

Resources in this definition refer to manpower, materials, time, etc., and the 'controlled' element is the way in which those resources are deployed taking into account legislation, company policies and so on.

The whole organization should be viewed as a series of processes from external suppliers to external customers. What frequently happens within companies, especially small businesses, is that processes are not well documented, if at all. As a result process problems cannot be identified and improved upon. Indeed in some organizations many processes could almost be viewed as a 'black art' in that they have evolved in intricacy over a number of years with no record of what they are or of their impact on the external customer.

Only by mapping processes within the company can the small business manager establish what exactly is going on. And only then, once the map has been drawn, can he or she begin improving processes so that the route to customer satisfaction is more direct and barrier free.

The mechanism for recording business processes is via diagrammatic flowcharts. By the use of various symbols, process inputs and outputs, decision points and related activities can be recorded in a graphic and simple manner. Some examples of such flowchart symbols are shown in Figure 4.6. An example of an actual process using flow chart symbols is given in Figure 4.7.

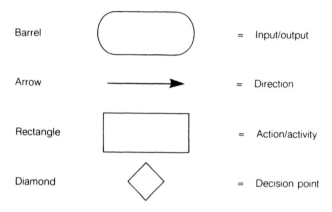

Barrel = Input/output

Arrow = Direction

Rectangle = Action/activity

Diamond = Decision point

Figure 4.6 Examples of flowchart symbols.

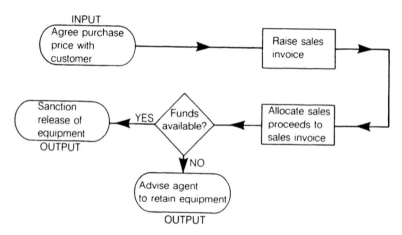

Figure 4.7 Example of a flowchart showing the sale of reprocessed stock.

The mapping of business processes can often prove a revelation. Overlap of functions or activity, blind alleys and extensive circumvention all reveal themselves when processes are recorded.

Obvious changes necessary to business processes may be put into effect immediately. We will see later (Chapter 8) how staff can be formed into corrective action teams and continuous improvement teams to streamline and improve upon internal processes.

4.5 CHAPTER SUMMARY

- A quality diagnosis is a prerequisite to quality improvement as it will establish a base point for implementing TQM.
- Do not assume in the absence of customer complaints or through informal contacts alone that customer requirements are being satisfied.
- Ask customers specific questions through the use of formal questionnaires about your company's current performance and its scope for improvement.
- Seek the views of staff through an opinion survey either in an anonymous questionnaire format or through group discussions using an outside facilitator.
- View the company as a series of processes converting inputs from suppliers to outputs for customers. Using flow diagrams map out each individual process as a preliminary to process improvement.

The cost of quality | 5

5.1 DEFINITION

The cost of quality can be defined as:

> The sum of the costs of everything that would not have been necessary if everything else was done right the first time.

Control of the cost of quality is one of the major benefits of implementing TQM. Many organizations concentrate on two areas when initiating Total Quality, namely the attainment of registration to Quality Assurance standard BS 5750/ISO 9000 or the satisfaction of customers through customer care programmes, customer surveys and the like. Such organizations disregard the fact that TQM can also lead to substantial cost savings. Increasing efficiencies and erradicating waste, through assessing and reducing the cost of Quality, can have a potent effect upon the cash flow and profitability of the small business.

In British manufacturing industry a number of studies have shown that the cost of quality is typically 25% of sales turnover. In the service industry it can be more akin to 40%. There are many companies that have managed to reduce the cost of quality by up to 90%. Consider the benefits to a small organization of a profit increase of nearly 40% of current turnover! By monitoring Quality costs, improvements to a company's products or services are achieved without spiralling cost increases.

Successful reductions to the cost of quality have been particularly dramatic in America. For example, Rank Xerox's Business Products and Systems organization achieved the following improvements by tackling its cost of quality:

- a reduction in the number of defects per machine by 78%, and
- a decrease in unscheduled maintenance by 40% and service response time by 27%.

As a result the company saved millions of dollars by first identifying the cost of quality and then undertaking corrective action to reduce it.

In elaborating upon the general definition above, the cost of quality can be separated into three categories, namely:

- the cost of conformance to customer requirements;
- the cost of non-conformance to customer requirements;
- basic operational costs.

Defining each element in turn, the **cost of conformance** is the cost an organization incurs in meeting the requirements of its customers. A strong element of this cost is the money a company spends on preventing products or services going wrong or checking that they are right before they reach the customer. The **costs of non-conformance** are failure costs, i.e. the costs incurred by a company in repairing what has gone wrong. The third category **basic operational costs** are the costs an organization cannot avoid encountering during the normal performance of its business. Diagramatically Quality costs and the benefit of their reduction can be represented as in Fig. 5.1.

Taking the cost of non-conformance first, failure costs to a company can be divided into external failure costs and internal failure costs.

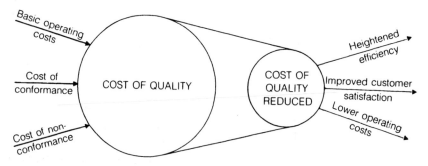

Figure 5.1 Benefits of reducing the cost of Quality.

External failure costs can be defined as follows:

Non-conformance costs that result from the discovery of defects or errors by the customer once the product or service has left the organization.

Examples of these costs could include:

- warranty adjustments
- repairs
- customer service
- faulty invoices
- product recalls
- returned goods
- returned repaired goods
- product liability litigation.

A significant external failure cost in addition to the examples quoted above is the lost opportunity cost and reduction in market share arising from a tarnished reputation.

Internal failure costs can be defined as follows:

Non-conformance costs that results from things going wrong during the process of manufacture or service provision which are detected before they reach the customer.

Examples of internal failure costs could include:

- scrap
- downtime caused by defects
- rework and repair
- re-inspection of rework
- excess inventory
- typing errors
- failure analysis
- downgrading because of defects.

In describing the cost of conformance I stressed that its principal component was **prevention costs**. Prevention costs can be defined as follows:

The cost of any activity undertaken by a company which prevents things from going wrong.

Examples of prevention costs could include:

- quality data collection
- quality improvement projects
- field trials
- market research
- quality planning
- quality education and training
- statistical process controls
- technical reviews.

The second element of the cost of conformance is **appraisal costs**. These costs can be defined as follows:

the costs of all the inspection and checking activities that occur within an organization to ensure that the product or service does not reach the customer in a defective state.

Theoretically these costs would be unnecessary if everything a company did was done right first time. Examples of appraisal costs could include:

- goods in inspection
- in-process inspection
- purchase order checking
- final inspection

- laboratory inspection
- quality audits
- financial audits
- calibration of quality measurement equipment.

Prevention costs should be viewed more as an investment. By investing in prevention activities, failure will not arise and the need for excessive appraisal costs will become superfluous.

5.2 WHY CALCULATE THE COST OF QUALITY?

This may seem an obvious question. However, the overriding reason to calculate the cost of quality is twofold:

- to reduce the costs of current operations;
- to prevent excess costs occurring when Quality improvement activities are implemented.

As we have seen in Chapter 4, the calculation of the cost of Quality is an additional diagnostic step in establishing current performance. An analysis of the cost of Quality is a convenient accompaniment to the business process analysis described in the previous chapter. By these two activities, particular processes will have been clarified and their current cost of quality established. Cost savings will therefore become a criterion in any process changes envisaged.

We have also seen that by incurring prevention costs, failure and appraisal costs will reduce substantially. The resultant savings to the company will enable it to invest further in the process of continuous improvement. This is of particular importance to the small business manager who may find the weight of unnecessary costs to be a burden when investing in TQM.

One of the principles of Kaizen, the Japanese word for continuous improvement, is the removal of waste. The Japanese regard anything which does not add value to a product or service as being an unnecessary cost. A cost of Quality analysis will act as a main vehicle for identifying non-added value activities and will assist the small business manager to reduce overheads to a minimum and decimate indirect costs. In this way anything which does not add value (i.e. what the customer pays for) will be exposed and eradicated. Such a perspective will also overcome the 'row faster, you swine' theory of management so that employees in the face of adversity do not necessarily have to work harder, but by engaging in more effective use of time – and methods and materials – will work 'smarter' for the benefit of both the individual and the organization as a whole. Removal of unnecessary costs in this way will make a company's goods and services more competitive and more profitable in that wasteful costs need not be passed on to the customer in increased prices so jeopardizing competitiveness (Figure 5.2).

By emphasizing the importance of the cost of Quality, the small business manager will have succeeded in heightening Quality-related activities giving it equal status to all the other activities such as marketing, production, R&D and the like within the business.

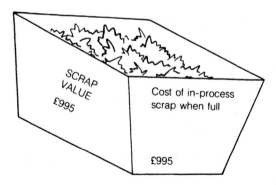

Figure 5.2 Highlighting the cost of Quality – a skip showing the cost of Quality when full.

61

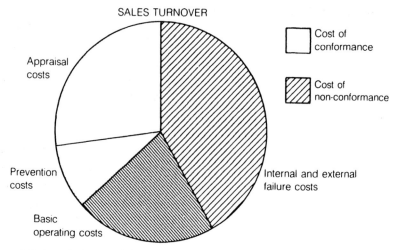

Figure 5.3 A typical cost of Quality profile.

Identifying the cost of quality will draw attention to activities of high cost. It will provide an effective measure of performance and will act as a good comparator for various processes, products and services and departmental performances.

Figure 5.3 shows a typical cost of Quality profile. As so little has been spent on prevention measures, non-conformance costs as a percentage of annual sales turnover are disproportionately high.

The following case study illustrates the benefits of quality cost measurement and reduction.

Case study: Calculating the cost of Quality

A company specializing in plastics technology realized that its operating costs were threatening its customer base and exposing it to increasing foreign competition. In undertaking a Total Quality drive the company embarked upon a major efficiency initiative by analysing its costs of Quality.

The initial analysis showed the cost of Quality to be some 22% of the company's annual turnover. More than half of those costs were internal failures in the form of scrap material and product defects. They were calculated by giving a sterling value to every non-conformance report which the workforce were encouraged to complete for every business process. In view of the high internal failure rate, appraisal costs were exceptionally high. At the time of the analysis, prevention costs – mainly attributed to research and development activities – were minimal in comparison.

The company's cost of Quality profile was altered dramatically when it began investing in prevention activities involving the creation of corrective action teams to correct errors and prevent mistakes re-occurring. Within six months non-conformances had fallen by nearly 40% with a resultant saving to the company of over £60 000.

One of the highest costs of quality are the indirect and often intangible costs associated with running the business, such as administration or customer services. Bad customer service, for example, can have both a high direct and high indirect cost, as can be seen in Table 5.1.

Table 5.1 The cost of bad customer service

Direct costs	Indirect costs
● Complaints handling	● Lost sales from those affected
● Costs of returns/refunds	● Lost potential sales of those informed of the service
● Costs of legal activities	● Cost of acquiring replacement customers
● Corrective PR	● Cost of lost opportunities to expand

5.3 HOW TO CALCULATE THE COST OF QUALITY

To commence the calculation of the cost of Quality the small business manager must engage the workforce in analysing all of their activities over a given period (say five working days), breaking down such activities into conformance and non-conformance activities. The cost of Quality champion nominated by the management team (see Chapter 3) in conjunction with the Quality manager and financial controller (if the latter is not actually the champion) could plan the activities of the exercise. For it to succeed, however, like everything else

COST OF QUALITY ANALYSIS   Key: BOC = Basic operating costs
DEPARTMENT: P   = Prevention costs
                                  A   = Appraisal costs
PERIOD: IntF = Internal failure costs
                                  ExtF = External failure costs

TIME RECORD

ACTIVITY	TIME	ANALYSIS					COQ*	ANNUALIZED
	HRS	BOC	P	A	INT F	EXT F	£	£
*COQ = Materials + Hourly rate × Time spent TOTALS								

Figure 5.4 A typical cost of Quality calculation form.

in TQM, its purpose must be communicated to the workforce, and standard documentation be designed for calculation purposes. An example of the type of assessment sheet used in cost of Quality analyses is given in Fig. 5.4.

As each member of staff calculates the costs of his or her activities over the given period, breaking them down into basic operational costs, prevention, appraisal and failure costs, plus any materials wasted (scrap), the cost of Quality calculation emerging from the trial period can be extrapolated to give an estimate of the annual cost of Quality for each individual department and for the company as a whole. Major failure costs will be highlighted in this way and will act as an incentive to focus corrective actions once TQM implementation commences.

The aim of the whole exercise is to achieve the cost profile depicted in Figure 5.5 in which, as a result of the increase in prevention costs, the overall cost of quality has reduced significantly.

Once the initial analysis has been undertaken, further analysis should be undertaken at, say, six monthly intervals to identify cost of Quality reductions as a result of TQM activities. The analyses should be communicated to the workforce regularly and displayed and updated on all works notices and discussed at team briefings. In communicating the cost of Quality exercise, the small business manager must take care that it is not construed as a means of

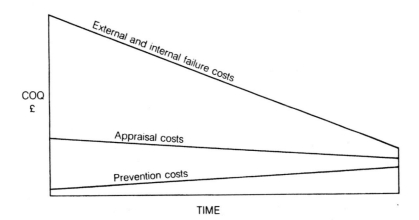

Figure 5.5 Cost of Quality reductions.

criticizing inefficiencies or threatening jobs. Viewed in such a light, people will deliberately conceal the real costs of Quality leaving the organization with an inaccurate view of its own efficiency.

Very often a cost of Quality committee is established and trained in the concepts and methodologies. Committee members will assist the remainder of the workforce in the calculations and, if selected on a departmental basis, be responsible to the cost of Quality champion for his or her department's input into the exercise. The following example taken from a public sector organization sets out one particular approach to calculating the cost of Quality.

Case study: Cost of Quality in a self-contained government organization

Cost of Quality (COQ) procedures

Introduction

Quality costing is a powerful technique used to monitor the real effect on the business of the cost of failing to achieve Quality requirements. When a Quality requirement is not achieved 'right first time' the full cost impact is attributed to non-conformance.

Non-conformances are measured in pounds (not numbers or percentages), as this enables effective priorities to be allocated and may be used as the justification for the cost of corrective action.

Corrective action is targeted to ensure that the process is refined and that the failure is not repeated. The technique may also be used to test the effect (in pounds) of any process change introduced.

Theory

The cost of a business process, whether research, manufacturing or administration, can be broken down into three elements:

- **Minimum process cost (MPC)***. This is the cost of the basic process with no verification or checking of output, and no rework.

*An alternative form for 'basic operational costs' used in this text.

- **Cost of conformance (COC)**. This is the money invested in prevention or checking to ensure that the requirements are met.
- **Cost of non-conformance (CONC)**. This is the cost of failing to get it 'right first time'.

The total cost of a process is the sum of all three elements. The COQ is the sum of the COC and the CONC, that is the money spent on the prevention or correction of faults.

$$\text{Total process cost} = \text{MPC} + \text{COC} + \text{CONC}$$
$$\text{COQ} = \text{COC} + \text{CONC}$$

Cost of Quality method

Before any study is initiated it must be supported by the manager of the area affected. The manager should lead the study and should seek advice from the Quality Implementation Team (QIT). The function of the Quality Implementation Team is to advise on how to gain the maximum benefit for the department or section in question. The results of all studies will be circulated to the Agency director and all departmental managers. This information may then be used to target problem-solving teams etc.

COQ techniques will also be used to monitor the cost of conformance and non-conformance on an annual basis to gauge the gross effect of the Total Quality programme. Studies will be conducted over as short a period as possible consistent with achieving a fair result (usually several weeks).

The data for the COQ study is gathered by everyone in the area under study filling in a time sheet and classifying everything they have done as one of the three cost elements (MPC, COC or CONC). The accuracy of the results depends on everyone involved being able to classify costs correctly. It is important that all staff receive relevant training and that they are tested in some way to ensure some uniform level of understanding across the area.

The aim of a COQ study is to gather data to help prioritize problem areas, not problem people. Management must make

67

it clear that staff will not be blamed for reporting a high level of non-conformance.

Procedure for COQ study

1. Choose an area or activity to be studied.
2. Choose a team to lead the study. The team should be lead by the manager of the area under study, since the data is for his/her initial benefit.
3. Prepare a cost model. The team should list the work processes carried out in the area and organize them into groups.
4. Brief staff. If the staff have not been involved in a COQ study before, then a short workshop or seminar to explain the theory will be required followed by some form of test to establish some level of confidence.
5. Gather data. Each individual records the time he/she has spent on each work process and classifies it as one of the three cost elements. The study team should act as a focal point for queries about categorizing work and should monitor staff to make sure they are filling in the sheets correctly and on time.
6. Process data. The times spent on each work process is converted into money by multiplying it by the charge rate for each individual's grade. The figures for each work process are then combined. The data is then passed to the study team for analysis.
7. Action. The results of investigation will be examined by the Quality Implementation Team together with any remedial recommendations. A plan of action will be put together by the study team and Quality Implementation Team which, subject to the director's approval, will be implemented forthwith.

COQ plan

In general there will be two distinct types of study, the annual organization-wide study and the targeted study.

- **The annual study**. There will be one general (all activities) study. The results will form a document that will indicate the general Quality trends within the Agency year to year. The Quality Implementation Team will scrutinize the results and recommend to the Agency director any specific or general actions required.
- **The targeted study**. These may be conducted within one or more departments but are targeted to no more than a few activities. Targeted studies may be initiated by any member of staff subject to the approval of the Quality Implementation Team. It may be based on the results of an annual study or as the result of some general concern.

Once the cost of Quality has been calculated for a given period, the information gathered will enable the small business manager to prioritize activities in the improvement process. This information coupled with all other sources of information form the diagnostic stage of TQM implementation. It will enable the small business manager to establish where to start.

5.4 CHAPTER SUMMARY

- Calculating the cost of Quality will act as an indicator of current efficiency.
- Reducing the cost of Quality will enable the improvement process to unfold without the burden of excessive additional costs.
- Knowing the cost of Quality will place a measure upon current business processes and highlight waste.
- The cost of Quality should be calculated over a given period using standard documentation with the involvement of the whole workforce. The costs calculated from this 'snapshot' can then be extrapolated to give an annual cost of Quality.
- The rationale for the cost of Quality should be communicated to the whole workforce beforehand and the result published.
- Improvement activities can be prioritized from the results of the exercise.

Customers and suppliers | 6

6.1 THE CUSTOMER

In a market economy, the cliché 'the customer is king' is well worn but never failing in its veracity. The whole purpose of TQM is customer satisfaction to such a degree that not only will his or her expectations be met, but will be exceeded and so 'delight' the customer – to quote Edwards Deming – that he or she will continue to place repeat business with the organization. Customer satisfaction should be the primary driving force of most, if not all, TQM initiatives. The aim of this chapter therefore is to demonstrate how small businesses can develop a customer orientation and, in so doing, build stronger relationships which provide high levels of customer retention and significant opportunities for increased sales.

Customers come in two forms: business customers where organizations engage in business-to-business transactions, and members of the public, whether they be random, as in the case of retail businesses, or selective, as, for example, in the case of medical and dental practices or local authorities. Irrespective of the type of customer one has, all organizations should be constantly rethinking their approach to their customers. A basic question for the small business manager to consider would be: 'Who are our customers?'

The retailers Marks & Spencer have answered this question as follows:

- A customer is the most important person in our business.
- A person who comes with needs and wants.
- A person with feelings who deserves to be treated with respect.

71

- The purpose of our work.
- A person deserving courtesy and attention.

In planning the implementation of TQM the small business manager can glean some information on whether his or her customers are being satisfied by undertaking a customer survey (Chapter 4). In dealing with the customer, one issue to beware of is the tendency for customer expectation to increase over time and for the supplier organization to gradually fall behind those expectations, thus creating a 'quality gap' between expectation and performance (Figure 6.1).

Many organizations are sadly unaware of the dimensions of the 'Quality gap' and are so surprised when they go out of business as a result. What the small business manager must do is convert the 'Quality gap', when known, into a 'Quality edge' by improving performance so that it not only meets but surpasses expectation.

Business process analysis (as described in Chapter 4) is the first step in establishing the reasons for current performance in that it will reveal how the process of converting vendor inputs performs *vis-à-vis* the requirements of the external customer. The 'Quality edge' will be obtained by process improvements plus the development of the internal customer/supplier (see section 5.2 below) so that a customer–supplier chain is created mirroring the business processes of the organization.

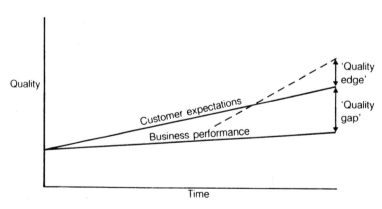

Figure 6.1 The 'Quality gap' and the 'Quality edge'.

It would be a mistake, however, to assume that the only mechanism for feedback on current performance should come via a customer survey. Information as regards performance can equally be gained from the face-to-face encounters between customer and supplier. The salesperson's meeting with the purchasing department of a customer would be an obvious point of contact for such information. A better approach to the informality of such associations would be for the small business manager to forge formal relationships between members of staff throughout his or her own business with their counterparts in a customer organization. One's customer counterpart could be as shown in Figure 6.2.

The relationships established in this way should not consist of just telephone or correspondence contact alone, but should involve regular face-to-face meetings. Through visiting each other's place of work, agreeing customer–supplier requirements and performance standards and working in cross-company teams to resolve problems, each may learn from the other and so continuously improve the relationship and the Quality of the product or service from the supplier to the customer. In adopting such an approach the small business manager will gain valuable information on how the organization is performing and will be able to draw comparisons against competitors.

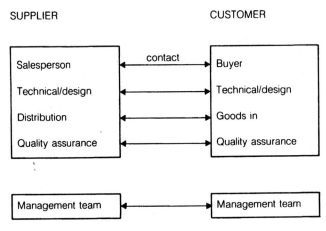

Figure 6.2 Customer–supplier relationships.

As with all other processes, the sales process should be recorded. Once it has been mapped measures to improve the process can be established. A continuous improvement team (see Chapter 7 for details) could be established within the organization and could also involve inputs from the customer (or a number of customers). In my experience when customers are asked to comment on performance and improvement in such a way, they will readily put forth constructive suggestions. After all, the customer organization itself stands to benefit and renewed confidence in the relationship will be formed.

Two key driving forces in improvement of the sales process should be the increase in sales volume and a reduction in the cost of sales. The formation of cross-departmental teams with an input into sales expansion and cost reduction should then be brought together to achieve these compatible objectives.

6.2 INTERNAL CUSTOMER–SUPPLIER CHAINS

For an organization to achieve a total customer orientation TQM requires that customer–supplier relationships are also brought in-house. As an organization seeks to satisfy its external customers' requirements, so the same philosophy can be internalized. Each department within the process flow treats its 'customer' department as if it were a highly valued customer. Equally, each individual becomes both an internal customer and supplier along the business process flow as shown in Figure 6.3.

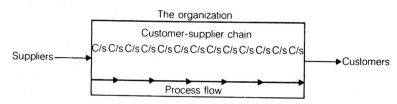

Figure 6.3 The customer/supplier chain.

Once a customer–supplier chain has been established, each individual customer should stipulate clearly and in writing what is required of his or her suppliers.

Each internal customer requirement will emanate from the requirements of the external customer. Performance will be set and measured between each customer and supplier. In this way not only will the service to the external customer be enhanced but relationships internally will become more effective. Monitoring of satisfaction levels along the customer–supplier chain will be one of the major advancements in continuous improvement. This can be best established by the introduction of statistical monitoring techniques, noticeably statistical process control (SPC) as detailed in Chapter 9.

Some examples of measures of performance that can be used in a customer/supplier chain are shown in Figure 6.4.

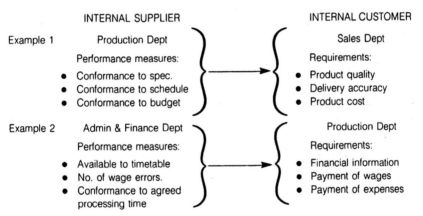

Figure 6.4 Two examples of performance measures in the customer/supplier chain.

Case study: Developing internal customer–supplier relationships

A company of 120 staff, operating as a manufacturer to the leisure industry, experienced continual problems between its salesforce and its production department. The problem in existence was a lack of understanding between the respective needs of each department. Frequently the salesforce would make promises to customers which when fed into the production facilities of the company caused all sorts of difficulties and animosities. Production would complain that the salesforce were making rash promises to customers to 'curry favour' which, when not fulfilled, would make the production department a convenient scapegoat for their own incompetence. The view of the salesforce in turn was that they were actively seeking and winning new orders but were frequently being let down by a production facility which was inflexible and cumbersome.

As part of the company's TQM drive, the company's managing director together with his head of sales and production decided to improve inter-departmental relationships by clarifying the business processes between production and sales and establishing a working customer–supplier relationship between the two departments. A first step, using an external consultant, was to review the processes currently in operation between the two departments. Meetings were then convened of a cross section of staff within each department, to 'let off steam' and comment on the attitudes and problems arising. Once a target list of issues had emerged, both departments were brought together to ratify the proposed change in the process and agree performance measures between the two departments. Moreover, a customer–supplier chain was established of individuals within and between each department. A customer/supplier working group was established, comprising representatives of both departments who agreed to meet on a monthly basis to review progress.

Throughout the process the remaining staff within production and sales were kept fully briefed as to the reasoning and operation of the chain. Suggestions for improvement were cultivated by both the sales and production directors with the active support of the managing director. The result of the exercise was a realistic understanding of the needs and wants of each respective department. Individual as well as departmental relationships were enhanced. Process changes enabled a far quicker production response time and also allowed the sales force to give customers confident production and delivery predictions when taking orders.

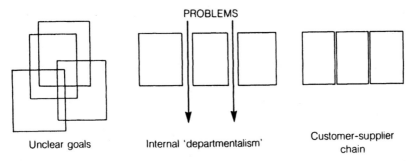

Figure 6.5 Departmental behaviour showing the benefits of the customer/supplier chain.

As shown in the above case study, one of the great benefits of an effective customer–supplier chain is to break down hostilities between departments, to clarify roles and objectives and to avoid waste and duplication of effort. Figure 6.5 illustrates the point.

In some organisations, the customer–supplier relationship has so solidified that formal 'partnership' agreements exists, entailing formal reviews and internal supplier assessments.

In a small business context, while not wishing to increase the levels of paperwork, some documentation will help formalize relationships within the business. An example of documentation actually in use – in this case an internal customer assessment form used by a financial organisation – is contained in Figure 6.6. It may help the small business manager establish a meaningful customer–supplier chain within his or her organization.

To make the customer–supplier chain work, the following steps should first be undertaken.

1. Agree and understand internal customer requirements.
2. Agree performance measures.
3. Record requirements and measures in documentary form.
4. Monitor conformance to requirements.
5. Conduct periodic performance reviews.
6. Highlight problem areas.

77

CUSTOMER/SUPPLIER CURRENT PERFORMANCE ASSESSMENT

SERVICE: PROCESSING OF CUSTOMER CORRESPONDENCE FOR

CUSTOMER: CENTRAL RECORDS.   MICROFILMING.

DATE: APRIL 93

REQUIREMENTS/ SERVICE STANDARDS.	Method of measuring and unit of measure	Current Performance
• CORRESPONDENCE SENT ON A DAILY BASIS VIA THE ENVOPAK	TICK SHEET	100% NO ERRORS
• CORRESPONDENCE BANDED WITH A BATCH HEADER, AND DEPT. TITLE ON FRONT.	TICK SHEET	100% NO ERRORS
• ALL CORRESPONDENCE IN THE BUNDLE HAVE THE SAME DATE OF DISPATCH.	TICK SHEET	100% NO ERRORS
• COMPUTER CODE ADDED CORRECTLY.	CONTROL CHART	93.7% 133 ERRORS PER 2138 ITEMS IN A SAMPLE.
• ACCOUNT NUMBER ON EVERY SHEET OF CORRESPONDENCE IN THE TOP RIGHT HAND CORNER.	CONTROL CHART	98.5% 30 ERRORS PER 2138
• MICROFILM DATE IN TOP RIGHT HAND CORNER OF CORRESPONDENCE	CONTROL CHART	97.5% 50 ERRORS PER 2138

CUSTOMER/SUPPLIER IMPROVEMENT AGREEMENT

*Delete as applicable

SERVICE: PROCESSING OF CUSTOMER CORRESPONDENCE FOR MICROFILMING	DATE: APRIL 93
CUSTOMER: CENTRAL RECORDS.	SUPPLIER: CUSTOMER SERVICES

SHORTFALL IN SERVICE REQUIREMENTS OR TARGET AREAS FOR IMPROVEMENT	Expected benefits from the improvement	Agreed Course of Action/Target Performance Improvement	Target Date
1. ABSENT OR INCORRECT COMPUTER CODE CORRESPONDENCE.	133 FEWER ERRORS PER MONTH CONC SAVING £34942.12 PER ANNUM	CODING CAN BE DONE BY CENTRAL RECORDS WHO HAD TO ACCESS THE SCREEN TO ADD FURTHER DETAILS ON THE CORRESPONDENCE. - ALL ERRORS ELIMINATED.	1.5.93
2. MICROFILM DATE IN TOP RIGHT HAND CORNER OF CORRESPONDENCE NOT ALWAYS IN THE RIGHT PLACE.	WITH NO FEWER ERRORS PER MONTH FOR INITIAL TARGET PONC SAVING £1185.60 p.a.	THE CHECKSHEET FOR PROCESSING CORRESPONDENCE IS TO BE UPDATED SPECIFYING THE LOCATION OF THE MICROFILM DATE. TARGET 99.5% 10 ERRORS PER MONTH	31.5.93
3. ACCOUNT NUMBER ON EVERY SHEET OF CORRESPONDENCE	POTENTIAL SAVING OF £889.20 p.a.	THIS ITEM IS ALREADY ON THE ABOVE CHECK SHEET. IT'S IMPORTANCE IS IS TO BE RE-EMPHASIZED AT THE NEXT TEAM MEETING AND CUSTOMER SERVICES ARE TO MEASURE THE PERFORMANCE AND AIM TO ELIMINATE ERRORS ACROSS THE NEXT 3 MONTHS.	1.7.93

Figure 6.6 Examples of internal customer–supplier assessment documentation.

7. Form customer–supplier cross-functional problem-solving teams to eliminate problems.
8. Instil a spirit of continuous improvement into the organization.

6.3 CUSTOMER CARE

For many organizations customer care is a much neglected area of TQM. It is practised mainly in retail organizations dealing directly with the public, whereas in fact it should form a part of every organization's TQM initiative. Many believe that only a glut of formal customer complaints indicate the need for customer care. This invariably results in a series of formal behavioural or 'smile' training courses for customer-facing staff. How many times has one entered a hotel or retail store to be welcomed by exactly the same greeting and behavioural patterns from every member of staff encountered – the result of an automaton-forming customer care programme? When presented with a problem, however, the veneer soon wears thin. Staff revert to type, become po-faced and unhelpful, infuriating the customer because of the deceit involved in the original contrived behaviour.

Customer care can be defined as follows:

Every activity which occurs within an organization that ensures that a customer is not only satisfied but retained.

It is as much to do with care of the employee as it is the customer. How can staff be expected to behave in an 'appropriate' manner to their customers when they themselves are treated by their employer in a totally different way? The esteem in which customer-facing staff are held by their employer and colleagues is a matter of great importance. An example of where this would be true is in a super-market environment.

The supermarket scenario

Supermarkets pride themselves on the quality of their products. They provide an environment for the consumer which is both convenient and congenial. However, the only staff encountering customers within a supermarket are the checkout staff at the payment tills. Such staff, depending on the opening hours of the particular shop, usually work inconvenient hours and are very often placed under considerable pressure through the volume of customers. It would be a mistake for the supermarket proprietor to hold these staff in low esteem or make their pay and conditions inferior to that of their colleagues or comparable staff nearby. If this mistake was in fact made, such staff would soon pass on their feelings of dissatisfaction for their employer in their attitude and behaviour towards the customer. The customer in turn would exercise choice and shop next time at another store. The proprietor seeing a drop in custom may arrange a programme of customer care training for the checkout staff. The enforced behavioural changes taught at such training events will be practised only in a strained manner back at the shop. This behaviour would become obvious and prove even more detrimental to the viability of the business. Customers would still desert and, more damagingly no doubt, tell others of their experience. They in turn would exercise the same choice.

The lessons to be learned from the 'supermarket scenario' are applicable to all small businesses. Everyone has an equally important role to play and should be regarded as being of equal worth. There should be no 'pecking order' to the organization. All staff should be recognized for their contribution. The successs of the business should be based on teamwork.

6.4 EXTERNAL SUPPLIERS

For many small businesses bought-in components and services very often account for the highest proportion of costs. How to reduce these costs and to improve the Quality of goods and services purchased is a matter worthy of considerable attention for the small business manager.

The whole thrust of this book so far has been to urge the small business manager to satisfy the customer. However, small businesses also need to develop a strategy as a customer to their own external suppliers. The Japanese were perhaps the first in the field to develop dependent relationships with favoured suppliers, whereby a strong bond was formed of mutual benefit to both parties. In such a relationship the customer organization would place all its requirements with its favoured supplier in return for consistent high-quality service. This concept has rapidly developed elsewhere. Many of the larger organizations in the West now have their own Quality standard which suppliers must satisfy in order to become and remain of favoured supplier status. Hewlett Packard, the Ford Motor Company and the Rover Group are just some examples of companies that apply stringent supplier assessments. Moreover, BS 5750/ISO 9000 is very often insisted upon as an external standard of Quality before companies become eligible as suppliers, as many a small business may well know to its cost.

The small business manager can also adopt a similar policy to his or her own suppliers whereby in return for favoured status the supplying organization is encouraged to develop a reliable quality assurance standard. However, a step beyond this is for the small business in the process of implementing TQM to assist its suppliers in the establishment of such principles. In this way a true partnership between customer and supplier is formed which reduces the trading barriers between both organizations so that not only will a supplier organization know the requirements of its small business customer but will also be assisted by the introduction of TQM in meeting such requirements. The closeness in a relationship that will be achieved by such a policy will result in increased understanding and mutual benefit for both customer and supplier. The small business manager, however, will need to temper this advice with the practicality of using his or her own resources in such activities. However, the improved costs that may result from such activities should be weighed up carefully before adopting a cavalier attitude towards suppliers. A policing attitude toward suppliers where visits and inspections are undertaken with little or no prior warning may well reveal mistakes and poor quality. The relationship, however, will be based upon fear and resentment. It will do little to enhance the cooperation, understanding or Quality of performance seen in a true partnership.

Nevertheless some formal measures must be established between customer and supplier, otherwise the relationship may become too comfortable. Such measures could include:

- accurate, measurable customer requirements (in writing);
- periodic customer–supplier Quality reviews;
- An examination of the supplier's Quality policy;
- Creation of customer–supplier continuous improvement teams.

6.5 COMPLAINTS HANDLING

As stated earlier, many organizations in my experience judge the level of customer satisfaction by the amount of formal complaints they receive. This is a grave mistake. Formal complaints represent the tip of the iceberg and to base one's customer satisfaction policies on the number incurred could well place a company on the road to ruin. For every one complaint received a potential complainant will have informed very many others of the level of Quality present (Figure 6.7). It has been estimated that 85% of disappointed customers never come back whereas satisfied customers continue to return, making repeat orders more profitable for the organization than winning new customers. Rather than be reactive, therefore, it is better for the small business manager to take the initiative as described in the early part of this chapter and actively seek the views of his or her customers on current performance, asking specific questions to gain specific factual responses.

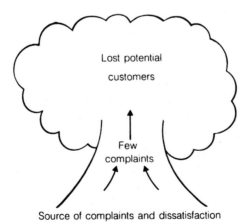

Figure 6.7 The 'nuclear' effect of poor Quality.

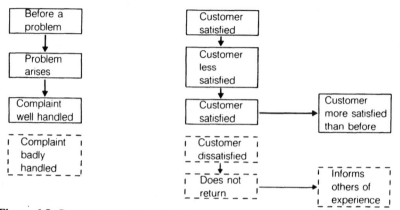

Figure 6.8 Customer complaints flowchart.

However, when complaints are received, if they are handled well then the customer may well become more satisfied with the supplier than before the complaint arose.

In addition, therefore, to seeking the views of the customer as to current performance, it is important for the small business manager to develop a complaints handling policy (Figure 6.8) as part of the TQM initiative.

The policy should ensure that when complaints do arise, they are dealt with quickly and efficiently and in such a manner that the customer is left feeling more satisfied than before the complaint first arose. Complaints should be actively encouraged and should be viewed as an opportunity for improvement rather than as negative criticism.

One final note on customer complaints – the customer is sometimes wrong. When this happens, the temptation is to apprise the customer of the fact in no uncertain manner. When tempted to do so, bear in mind the two golden rules of Stew Leonard Stores in the USA, one of the paragons of excellence in customer satisfaction:

Rule 1 The customer is always right.
Rule 2 If the customer is wrong, refer to rule one.

6.6 CHAPTER SUMMARY

- Customer satisfaction should be the primary driving force of TQM.
- As a first step, analyse who the customers are and assess what problems they experience.
- The company should cooperate with the customer to resolve the problems experienced.
- One-to-one relationships should be formed between the company and its customers.
- Analysis of the sales process should be undertaken to enhance customer satisfaction, and also to increase sales volume and reduce costs inherent in the process.
- The concept of customer satisfaction should be 'internalized' within the company to give a 'human face' to business processes.
- Customer care initiatives are an important facet of TQM but should be an integral part of employee care rather than stand alone in the form of behavioural training for customer contact staff.
- An organization should encourage complaints as an opportunity for improvement.
- As customer relations are of great importance, relationships between the company and its own suppliers carry equal weight.
- Active partnerships between the small business and its suppliers should be formed.

Leadership | 7

7.1 A TYPICAL SCENARIO ...

An entrepreneur with an interesting idea produces a prototype at home or in spare time at work. With great excitement he undertakes market research into the commercial viability of his product, forms an attractive business plan and after lengthy persuasion of his bank manager, gains financial backing. He resigns his job and recruits his immediate family to grow the embryonic business. After perhaps some early setbacks, the venture proves successful, justifying the risk of leaving secure employment. In time non-family employees are recruited – initially on the shop floor to work alongside the entrepreneur himself. The business continues to thrive. The entrepreneur's wife becomes company secretary or financial manager, the children take a leading role in managing the production operations while perhaps the youngest child is placed in charge of the administration function controlling a few clerical and typing staff.

Success is established. Communication with the workforce is easy and informal. Sales are sound and financial reward for the founder and his family as well as his loyal workforce, while not extravagant, is sufficient to justify undertaking the enterprise. Perhaps with the encouragement of the bank or local business advisors, the entrepreneur decides to expand and diversify. He employs a new general manager. He devotes his time to promoting the business in the dual role of managing director and sales director.

More staff are taken on. New systems for efficiency are introduced. Quality controls are applied, job descriptions are written. Cost controls are instituted to preserve healthy cash flow. Many of the staff perquisites and informal arrangements are curtailed in the interests of increased productivity. Absenteeism levels, once very low, increase. Quality standards fall, commitment deteriorates. A trusted employee who joined the company at the very outset leaves for a larger competitor, complaining that the company is no longer the employer it used to be. The entrepreneur finds that he has to spend more of his time concentrating on internal issues to the detriment of his external sales activities. He becomes increasingly fraught, trying to maintain external sales while running the business from the shop floor as he always used to. Tension at home increases. The general manager fails to live up to expectation. A major customer withdraws a lucrative order because of late deliveries. Inexorably the business goes into decline.

Such a scenario, often fulfilled, threatens the viability of many small businesses, through the inability of its founder to move from a hands-on practitioner, relying on technical expertise alone, to a competent business manager.

Problems of this nature are often overcome by sound leadership skills.

7.2 LEADERSHIP AND QUALITY

To manifest leadership qualities, the small business manager must visibly demonstrate commitment and conviction in the promotion of TQM. As stated earlier many organizations make the mistake of handing over Quality matters to the Quality manager, or treating it as a bolt-on to some other policies being pursued. If this occurs, then staff themselves will view Quality as a secondary issue to be taken up when other priorities have been dealt with. The small business manager must accept overall responsibility for the success of Quality improvement.

Leadership style is the epitomy of the company culture needed for an organization to make a success of TQM. The small business manager must proclaim his or her vision for the company. The staff must be excited and motivated in such a way as to achieve commitment and willing cooperation. Praise, encouragement, developing teamwork, 'creating the conditions' for excellence are all examples of sound leadership. No less important is the need to remove fear from the organization. The small business manager in his or her leadership style should encourage staff to adopt a preparedness to innovate, experiment and improvise in the quest for improvement.

One of the distinguishing features of companies dedicated to TQM is the positive atmosphere that pervades the organization. To practise TQM the small business manager believes in delegating as much of the decision-making as possible. Employees are able to take responsibility for their jobs and are involved in the decision-making process. They are allowed the freedom to solve problems that affect their daily working routine themselves or to call on the assistance of others when in doubt. Supervisors and managers are seen in a supportive role, helping and advising the workforce on ways of improvement. Communications are free flowing, suggestions and innovations are frequent. Such a culture is personified by the leadership style of the small business manager. He or she practises an open-door policy, actively encouraging all employees to come forward to discuss business issues. One of the key attributes of such a leadership style is to listen and not to force through personal ideas at every opportunity. Such a manager considers it a privilege to have staff prepared to spend forty hours and more of their weekly lives contributing to the success of the enterprise.

When supervisors act as controllers, telling employees what to do at every turn, staff feel powerless, morale suffers, job satisfaction deteriorates. The events of the scenario described above are set in train and the business frequently declines and fails.

Case study: Leadership style and principles

A city-based finance house, part of a multinational group but independently managed and employing 80 staff, decided to convene an off-site workshop. With the facilitation of an external consultant, the workshop determined the principles of leadership and agreed an appropriate leadership style for its senior management team to adopt as part of the company's TQM initiative.

The following leadership principles were agreed on as part of the TQM process:

- People are most committed to decisions they make themselves.
- Goals motivate both individuals and teams.
- Differences in status and conditions of service undermine achievement.
- Knowledge of results improves performance.

The workshop also produced a list of leadership characteristics to be adopted by each member of the management team:

- self-belief
- single-mindedness

- team-builder
- change-maker

- source of inspiration
- in possession of a clear vision
- persuasiveness
- good listener.

Each manager present at the workshop developed a personal action plan to fulfil the agreed leadership style.

The source of success, embodied in TQM, is for the small business manager to retain the informality which created the good fortune of the business at the start while developing sufficient trust in the staff to break away from internal issues to an external customer focus. He or she can do much to promote the prosperity of the business by creating a clear vision and effective teamwork and delegation, coupled with a concern and appreciation for each individual staff member's contribution.

Once the correct attitude of mind and patterns of behaviour have been established, the small business manager can prioritize activities, plan ahead and relinquish the daily fire-fighting that typifies businesses where employees are unable to take full responsibility for their work.

The late Douglas McGregor, Professor of Industrial Relations at the Massachusetts Institute of Technology, developed two contrasting theories about human motivation – Theory X and Theory Y* – which should be borne in mind by the small business manager when developing an appropriate leadership style.

* McGregor, D. (1985) *The Human Side of Enterprise*, New York, McGraw-Hill.

Theory X

1. The average human being has an inherent dislike of work and will avoid it if he can.
2. Most people must be coerced, controlled, directed, threatened with punishment to get them to put forth adequate effort toward the achievement of organizational objectives.
3. The average human being prefers to be directed, wishes to avoid responsibility, has relatively little ambition and above all wants security.

Theory Y

1. The expenditure of physical and mental effort in work is as natural as play or rest.
2. External control and the threat of punishment are not the only means for bringing about effort toward organizational objectives. Man will exercise self-direction and self-control in the service of objectives to which he is committed.
3. Commitment to objectives is a fraction of the rewards associated with their achievement.
4. The average human being learns, under proper conditions, not only to accept but to seek responsibility.
5. The capacity to exercise a relatively high degree of imagination, ingenuity and creativity in the solutions of organizational problems is widely, not narrowly, distributed in the population.
6. Under the conditions of modern industrial life, the intellectual potentialities of the average human being are only partially utilized.

Contrast the Theory Y beliefs with the Theory X view that staff are inherently work-shy and in need of constant supervision and instruction. In such organizations regulations and controls abound. Jobs are simplified to such an extent that little imagination or innovation is needed.

Few companies practising TQM adopt a Theory X style of leadership.

A useful exercise for the small business manager to undertake personally, and for his or managers to undertake with their staff, is r's Role in TQM

, our subordinates and ask them to complete the following exercise.

(1 = low 5 = high)

Please tick

	1	2	3	4	5
1. Classifying the job and stating the standard of performance expected					
2. Providing the means to do an effective job in terms of materials, techniques and procedures					
3. Instructing and imparting knowledge on the requirements to do a good job					
4. Empowering the jobholder to do his or her job without interference					
5. Recognizing and rewarding achievement and effort					
6. Encouraging effort					
7. Helping the jobholder to overcome difficulties when they occur					
8. Leading by example					

Figure 7.1 The manager's role in TQM.

illustrated in Figure 7.1. The results of this exercise will prove invaluable in determining the current management style, and will help develop a new style of management embracing the principles of sound leadership.

7.3 LEADERSHIP AND COMMUNICATION

Good leadership practice is maintained by sound methods of communication. However, one of the most commonly occurring problems besetting all business is the effectiveness of its communications. This is no less so in the case of the small business, especially in the course of its development from a survival strategy to a strategy for growth. Frequently the small business manager finds that more and more demands are placed on his or her time in terms of resolving day-to-day crises. 'If only people would talk to each other more' becomes a frequent refrain. But while an open-door policy is admirable, it is not enough to overcome the problem of communications for a business employing perhaps in excess of twenty staff.

An effective method of formal communications that could be introduced from the very start is one of team briefing. It is based on the idea of regular meetings between groups of staff cascading from the senior management team down throughout the organization. Team briefing is widespread in many large companies and is generally considered to be the most appropriate means of regular face-to-face communication. It operates on the following principles:

1. Board of directors/senior management team meet on a weekly or monthly basis. A 'core' brief is produced at each board meeting comprising information on such issues as new orders, production statistics, sales figures, new recruits/departures, future plans, etc.
2. Each board member briefs his or her immediate team of managers, adding where appropriate issues of local interest.
3. Each manager in turn briefs his or her team of supervisors, adding to the core brief more and more localized information.
4. Finally, each supervisor briefs his or her work team using the core brief as the central focus with relevant departmental and sectional issues added where necessary.

At each stage of the team briefing procedure, observations and feedback are encouraged, recorded and reported upwards. The timespan between the board meeting and the final stage of the briefing procedure should take place in as short a time as possible. In many organizations, the briefing cycle can take as little as 24 hours to run its full course. However, by using a standard written brief throughout, there is little opportunity for exaggeration or misrepresentation of information between different sections or departments. The fact that feedback is encouraged and reported at each stage also ensures that the top of the company is well informed of all shop-floor developments.

Obviously the tiers of the briefing system will need to be curtailed, depending on the size of the organization. For the very smallest companies, perhaps one or two levels of briefing will be needed at most. Team briefing meetings should be run to strict guidelines and be of limited duration. If not, there is a tendency for them to degenerate into 'gripe sessions' or a general free-for-all. Such a system, however, if well managed, should do much to overcome poor communications as a small business expands.

The benefits of team briefing are:

- face to face communications
- immediate feedback

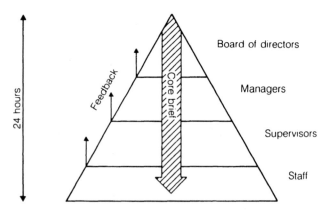

Figure 7.2 The theory of team briefing.

- a consistent message
- information of local relevance
- development of team spirit
- simplicity of organization.

Despite the value of team briefing, the small business manager's own visibility is still an important aspect of leadership and communications. Witness Montgomery's unflagging troop visits during the Africa Campaign of the Second World War, or Sir Colin Marshall's exhaustive employee briefings during the course of the 'Putting People First' British Airways quality initiative as examples of this. By 'walking the job' wherever possible, the small business manager, despite the growing success of the business, can do much to retain the personal touch that so much characterized the early days of the company. The small business manager should also encourage his or her immediate managers to adopt similar practices to support the formal briefing system and bolster the open communications culture that characterizes thriving organizations.

7.4 LEADERSHIP AND RECOGNITION

A third important aspect of good leadership (covered more fully in Chapter 11) lies in recognition and reward. The small business manager seeking to lead his or her firm to success should not only adopt the correct attitude of mind, communications stance and visibility, but should also be prepared to recognize good work at every opportunity. Recognition does not simply involve a pay rise or increased bonus for work well done – although this in itself is often a powerful source of motivation – but also includes recognizing achievement by the use of praise. While taking decisive action to correct any mistakes, a handshake, a letter of appreciation or merely a personal 'thank you' for good effort is very often all that is needed to develop a sense of loyalty and increased motivation. It is one of the fundamental behavioural attributes of good leadership.

7.5 LEADERSHIP AND SUPERVISION

An important consideration of the good leader is not to alienate middle management or first line supervisors. A pitfall often encountered is for the small business manager to encourage direct contact with the workforce, and in so doing, to disaffect or circumvent managers and supervisors. Such a course of action is likely to cause resentment and alienation. No matter how charismatic the individual business manager he or she will need to rely on supervisory staff to implement TQM. Without their commitment, TQM could be viewed as a threat to their own security and will not be implemented properly. At the planning stage, managers should be involved, understand and be committed to the TQM concept. Thereafter the leadership style adopted by the small business manager can be reflected by the supervisory staff to the general benefit of the enterprise.

7.6 CHAPTER SUMMARY

- Visible commitment to TQM must be a first priority for the small business manager.
- An open, trusting leadership style should be adopted and practised throughout every level of supervision.
- A belief that people are work-shy and uncooperative will prove self-fulfilling to the detriment of the business.
- Leadership style must be flexible to meet the particular needs of the moment.
- Communication on a formal basis is ensured by regular team briefing.
- The small business manager should still maintain visibility with the workforce 'walking the job' wherever possible.
- Recognition and praise are important attributes in the motivation of staff.
- Beware of the danger of alienating supervisors through not involving them in the TQM process.

Teamwork

8

8.1 TEAM DYNAMICS

A team can be defined as a group of individuals working in harmony to achieve a common objective which as individuals they would not have been able to achieve. Teamwork is one of the underlying principles of Total Quality. We have already established that the small business manager should examine his or her business on the basis of a process, or number of processes, for delivering customer satisfaction. For such processes to work it is important to instil cooperation between individuals and departments through the establishment of internal customer/supplier linkages and also to introduce a team-based approach to quality improvement.

In all spheres of activity the cooperation and shared understanding of a group of people with a common objective will usually achieve more than single individuals. This is no less the case with TQM. A team-based approach to quality improvement will create both a greater sense of purpose and mutual dependence. It is worth noting, however, that not all groups of individuals are necessarily exercising the characteristics of a team. There may be a common goal in many cases but not necessarily a mutual dependence or high level of collaboration. Indeed the small business manager in examining the groupings within the organization may discover that what were thought to be teams were in fact groups of individuals striving against each other in competition.

In the planning stage of TQM the need to create a common goal by the formation of a company mission was established. If the company is to act as a team to achieve that goal, it is the responsibility of the small business manager to ensure his or her company operates as a single team – in other words to develop a 'war spirit' where there is a common goal of survival or success and that everyone stands to gain or lose in the ensuing battles. Continuing the military metaphor, it is far better to meet a common enemy, i.e. one's competitors, on a united front than waste energy and resources on internal conflicts within the organization that will create company politics, a blame culture and mutual suspicion.

The team-building skills of the small business manager will be of vital importance in establishing a team-based culture. Professor John Adair in his Action Centred Theory of Leadership* has a model which will apply very aptly in developing a team-based approach to implementing TQM. He states that effective leadership rests on three premises, i.e. task, team and individual (Figure 8.1).

The small business manager along with other senior managers responsible for team building should be aware of Adair's leadership model and bear the following points in mind when developing teams.

- The objective of the team should be clearly stated and agreed.
- The approach to achieving a task should be based upon effective teamwork.

Figure 8.1 John Adair's action centred leadership

*Adair, J. (1983) *Effective Leadership* Aldershot, Gower.

- The leader of each team should be sensitive to the individual needs of each team member.

Team objectives should have the following characteristics:

- They should be agreed by the whole team.
- They should be written unambiguously so that everyone is clear as to the team's purpose.
- Measurable results need to be built into the objectives to that the team has a measure for success.
- As in any objective-setting exercise the team's objectives should be achievable with effort. Easy objectives will not stimulate the team sufficiently, while impossible objectives will demotivate individuals to the detriment of team cohesion.

Signs of effective teamwork within an organization will be the competent conduct of meetings, sound inter-departmental relationships, cross-functional teams and collective loyalty of staff to the company as a whole.

In considering a team-based approach to TQM, the small business manager should ask his or herself four fundamental questions:

- What teams currently exist within the organization?
- Do they have a purpose?
- Is each team effective at achieving its purpose?
- If not, why not?

It may be found that some of the teams in existence are now defunct and should be disbanded. Others may need rejuvenating by redefining their role and perhaps changing their composition by introducing new members to the team to induce new ideas. Undoubtedly many teams will need to be formed as I describe below, to resolve problems (corrective action teams) and to foster a spirit of continuous improvement (continuous improvement teams).

Especially within very small companies, team members will be required to fulfil a number of roles. Team leader is an obvious role. Four other categories of team member should also be included in the makeup of the team if it is to be successful (Figure 8.2).

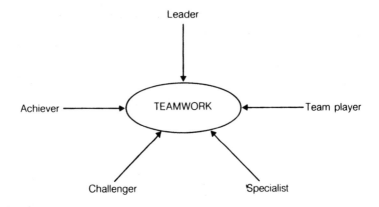

Figure 8.2 Five roles for effective teamwork.

- **Specialist.** An individual with an expert knowledge within a particular field, so that the team has the necessary expertise to fulfil its purpose.
- **Achiever.** This is an individual who is constantly monitoring the progress of the team against the targets set, urging team members to take action to achieve its objectives.
- **Team player.** An individual who is concerned about the effectiveness of the team from the stance of interpersonal relationships. This role is often portrayed by a meticulous, sensitive person who is conscientious in recording minutes and agreed actions of the team.
- **Challenger.** This is a confrontational role portrayed by an individual who does not fear to question some of the targets and assumptions of the team. The challenger role is played by a team's 'devil's advocate'.

Whereas some roles must be played by one individual (e.g. team leader), other roles for effective teamwork could be combined in the same individual. However, if one particular role predominates then the team will not be successful.

Case study: Effective teamwork

A small manufacturing company was being pressurized by the founding family to achieve greater results and profitability. In

100

response, an outside consultant was called in to examine the structure and roles of the management team to establish whether the company's operating systems or its personality mix was the cause of under-performance.

Operating procedures proved satisfactory on examination. However, when an analysis of each individual management team member's profile was undertaken, using a standard team analysis technique, it was found that without exception each member of the team fulfilled the role of 'team player'. No wonder the management team showed little achievement – no leader, no challenger, no specialist input. A new management team was the only course of action to bring the company back into profitability.

As in this case study, if the small business manager finds that some of the teams within his or her company are not effective because of an imbalance of role, then the makeup of the team must be changed to instil the necessary elements of success. Such an approach is as appropriate for his or her own management team as it is for every other team within the organization.

In terms of team size, five to eight people are an ideal number to maximize individual contributions. A larger number than eight will intimidate some of the more retiring team members and be dominated by more vociferous individuals present. Teams of less than five usually lack the combination of talents and ideas that a well balanced group can produce. Discussions within very small groups can prove arid and fruitless resulting in the group making little or no progress.

It is important that teams within the organization are not regarded as the 'chosen few'. The small business manager must comunicate the fact that TQM is based on teamwork and that everyone, sooner or later, will be involved in team–based activities. With the initial teams, the small business manager should take every opportunity to ensure that other members of the department in question are kept fully informed of the team's progress and that the team members actively discuss the team's developments. An approach of this nature will avoid feelings of alienation by those not involved in team activities and should ensure a more ready acceptance of the team's recommendation.

Figure 8.3 Elements of effective teamwork.

The elements necessary for effective teamwork are summarized in Figure 8.3.

8.2 TEAM DEVELOPMENT

In developing a team-based approach to continuous improvement, the small business manager should exercise patience in allowing newly formed teams time to achieve. Studies conducted on team behaviour reveal that each team goes through four distinct stages in its development. Charles Handy's team development analysis as stated in his book *Understanding Organizations** is perhaps the most well known. It runs as follows.

1. **Forming.** At the creation of a team, teamwork does not exist. The team *per se* is a group of individuals. During this phase of a team's development, matters like team purpose, team member roles, acceptance of team leader's authority and so on are still in the process of being formed.

*Handy, C. (1976) *Understanding Organizations*, Harmondsworth, England, Penguin Books.

102

2. **Storming.** This stage of the team development sequence is where initial agreements and role allocations are challenged and re-established. Hostilities and personal needs often emerge during this stage of development.
3. **Norming.** By now formal and informal relationships will have been established within the group. The process of decision-making will develop. Openness and cooperation are signs of the team's behaviour.
4. **Performing.** Having passed through the three previous stages, only then will a group operate in a successful manner. Trust, openness, healthy conflict and decisiveness are all aspects of a group's performance once it has reached this level of maturity.

After a team has reached the final stage in its development the small business manager should be aware that the team's performance may deteriorate unless its purpose remains clear and its members are still committed to fulfilling its purpose.

8.3 TEAMWORK AND LEADERSHIP STYLE

The team leader, to be successful, should be flexible in his or her leadership style. Without dominating team behaviour, the leader should vary his or her approach to deal with circumstances as they arise. As a team develops, so the team leader can facilitate the development by the adoption of the appropriate leadership style. The four stages of leadership which promote the development of teams are as follows.

1. **Directing.** Where tasks are allocated to team members and their performance monitored.
2. **Coaching.** Still taking strong lead but also involving the team members in the decision-making process.
3. **Facilitating.** This role supports others to achieve the tasks of the team. Responsibilities and decision-making are shared within the group.
4 **Delegating.** Decision-making is now within the authority of the group. The team leader, while retaining responsibility, has delegated authority to the team as a whole to decide itself on appropriate actions.

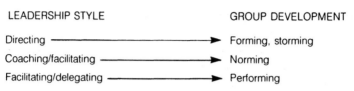

LEADERSHIP STYLE   GROUP DEVELOPMENT

Directing ⟶ Forming, storming

Coaching/facilitating ⟶ Norming

Facilitating/delegating ⟶ Performing

Figure 8.4 The relationship between leadership and team behaviour.

Figure 8.4 shows the close correlation between the four leadership styles and the development in a team's effectiveness.

When a team has reached such a level of maturity that the leadership style of the team is 'delegatory', then even the role of team leader may be changed enabling members of the team to adopt greater responsibility for the success of the team.

Some of the qualities of a good team leader include:

- honesty
- fairness
- trust
- stability
- openness
- job knowledge
- friendliness
- resolution.

Although these traits are innate in some people, they can be acquired. The small business manager should set an example to the rest of his or her colleagues by portraying such behavioural patterns, and should develop a company culture which encourages and rewards this behaviour in others.

In considering the role of the team leader in greater depth, it is the small business manager's ultimate responsibility to ensure that the team achieves its task. We have seen the flexibility of style and characteristics of an effective team leader and we have also examined the combination of personalities in the creation of a successful team. Nevertheless, team leaders will at some time be responsible for a team which will not make progress. Under such circumstances, the team leader should either seek consensus on a different objective, change some of the team players or in fact dissolve the whole team and form a new one. Problem-solving processes and problem-solving tools and techniques described in Chapter 9 will be an important characteristic of most teams formed by TQM. The team leader should ensure that he or she operates by agreement and encourages each individual member of the team to make a contribution.

8.4 ROLE OF THE FACILITATOR

Many organizations when implementing TQM train a number of selected individuals to act as TQM facilitators. Using a literal translation from the Latin, their role is to 'make things easier'. The role of facilitator is to support the team leader, and monitor the team's progress. A facilitator should be not only skilled in guiding teams but should also be well versed in TQM. We saw earlier in the book (Chapter 3) that the Quality manager should have a thorough grounding in Total Quality. Equally, team facilitators should be sufficiently well versed to resolve matters of approach or technique which may emerge during the course of a team's activity. Very often a team facilitator may be tempted to take control of a meeting if he or she sees it going awry. It is far better to leave the team to struggle through and only intervene as a last resort. A useful activity for the facilitator is to evaluate with the team the success of each meeting, asking the questions: 'What went well?' 'What was achieved?' 'What could be improved?'

Many small organizations combine the role of facilitator with that of Quality manager. In larger organizations – say of one hundred staff or more – or companies of a number of scattered locations, a number of team facilitators are established.

8.5 QUALITY IMPLEMENTATION TEAM

It has already been established that successful TQM is based on effective teamwork. However, random teamwork, no matter how competent, is not enough. There is a need for a formal team structure in the organization. The small business manager should therefore consider the formation of a Quality implementation team when implementing TQM.

In all but the very smallest of businesses, TQM cannot be planned and coordinated without the formation of a Quality implementation team. This is probably the most important team to form when contemplating the introduction of TQM. Its role is to take on overall responsibility for the execution of TQM within the organization. It is no good, however, to form this team from junior ranks of the organization. This will merely reflect the low status and priority attributed to Total Quality and will be viewed accordingly by the rest of the workforce. If TQM is to be the number one priority within an organization, then the Quality implementation team must comprise the company's board management. Under the personal leadership of the small business manager, each member of the Quality implementation team should be assigned a role within TQM to 'champion' (see Chapter 3 for more details of the various champion roles of the management team).

As a group the Quality implementation team should lead by example. All too often in business, boards of directors coerce or cajole their staff to behave in a particular manner while they themselves act in a completely different way. The Quality implementation team must 'live and breathe' TQM if it is to be successful lower down the company. Only in this way will sceptics and cynics be won over and conform to the new way of thinking.

The role of senior managers as a Quality implementation team is to control and plan the introduction of TQM. Only an implementation team of the company's senior managers can 'span' the whole of the organization so that if problems do emerge between different departments within the company, this team will have the overall authority and breadth of control to resolve them. The team should also act as the main body within the company for recognizing and rewarding the achievement of others in implementing TQM.

As stated before, the implementation of TQM must be driven from the top of the company. Expecting Total Quality to happen without any direction or guidance will prove futile. We have already seen that the small business manager, in motivating his or her senior team, could allocate one of the more important roles of TQM (e.g. education and training) to a team colleague suspected of not being fully committed to the concept.

One final point in discussing the role of the Quality implementation team is that every initiative within TQM should have the collective support and responsibility of the whole team. If this is not the case, certain issues or areas of TQM may be marginalized to the detriment of the whole initiative.

8.6 CORRECTIVE ACTION TEAMS (CATs)

As already established, a basic step for the small business manager undertaking TQM is to identify the current level of quality within the organization. Indicators of the current level of quality may be obtained from customer and staff surveys, or business process and cost of Quality analyses. Corrective action teams, as their name implies, are teams constituted to resolve problems. In the early stages of TQM they can be put to good use resolving the problems which emerge from such surveys of current Quality. They are supervisor- or manager-led and are made up of some four to six individuals who work in close proximity to the problem in question. Team members would therefore comprise either staff from one department or a number of departments concerned with the problem area or business process under consideration.

Corrective action teams have a specific remit and lifespan. Using the problem-solving methodologies and techniques described in Chapter 9 and Appendix B they will define and analyse the problem in question and then recommend corrective measures and solutions to the management board of a company or quality implementation team with a view to resolving the matter.

A presentation to the board should include the following:

- a definition of the problem and the resultant poor Quality;
- specific data to demonstrate the magnitude of the problem;
- solutions considered with their advantages and disadvantages;
- the preferred solution with expected benefits;
- a plan of implementation.

Corrective action teams are a powerful way of making progress with TQM. In time they will become a way of life for the small business. The small business manager may also consider forming a corrective action team before much of the Quality analysis has been undertaken to give initial impetus to TQM. 'Quick wins', as these activities are often referred to, are placed in the context of a TQM implementation programme in Chapter 12. Criteria which should be adopted in forming such early corrective teams include the following (Figure 8.5).

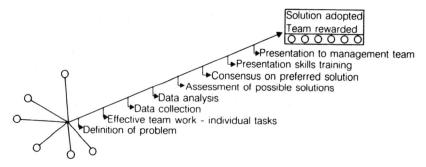

Figure 8.5 Corrective action team process.

- Select a problem which is well known and fairly easy to resolve.
- Select a team of people from the workforce who are bright and positive towards TQM.
- Communicate the need for corrective action to the remainder of the workforce.
- Give the team a high profile within the company.
- Implement the proposed solution to the problem wherever practicable.
- Publicize the results and savings or benefits to the company.
- Praise and congratulate the team for a job well done.
- Use the success and kudos of the first CAT team to stir up enthusiasm and support for TQM.
- Do not leave it too long before creating further CATs.

Case study: Corrective action teams

An electrical switch assembly supplier experienced problems concerning the printing of product details on a particular switch case. The problem arose from the feed mechanism to an ink jet printer.

A corrective action team was formed comprising line assembly workers under the team leadership of the line supervisor. By the application of the problem-solving process described in Chapter 9, the problem was defined, data was collected by examining parts returned internally and from the company's external customers, and the frequency of faults accruing was recorded by the use of check sheets at the point of printing.

The corrective action team assessed the data recorded over a period of one month and devised a number of possible solutions to the problem. Initial solutions included changing the diameter of the feed belt and altering the speed of the feed mechanism, neither of which worked in field trials. A new solution was proposed involving the use of a grip feed mechanism to increase the stability of each component to allow better print application. A new grip feed was designed by the team and a prototype feeder was manufactured by the jet printer suppliers.

Trials proved very successful reducing printing errors significantly. A presentation was made to the company's management team. The CAT's recommendations were approved by the management team resulting in the prototype grip feeder being applied to all of the jet printers on site. Printing errors were reduced by over 90%, leading to considerable financial savings for the company and a great deal of kudos for the corrective action team in question.

8.7 CONTINUOUS IMPROVEMENT TEAMS (CITs)

There is a distinct difference in concept between teams formed to put things right (CATs) and teams formed for the purpose of continuous improvement. The former involves resolving problems that have come to light from the various audits undertaken at the introduction of TQM or which emerge later during the course of implementation. They are designed to bring processes under control and eradicate one-off problems occurring. Continuous improvement teams are concerned with ameliorating processes or activities which are not producing immediate problems but which have scope for improvement to meet customer's (both internal and external) requirements. Figure 8.6 shows the difference in activity between corrective action teams and continuous improvement teams, whereby the CAT addresses problems occurring beyond the tolerance levels set (or customer requirements agreed) and the CIT focuses its attention on improvements to a process which is already operating to a satisfactory level with agreed tolerances.

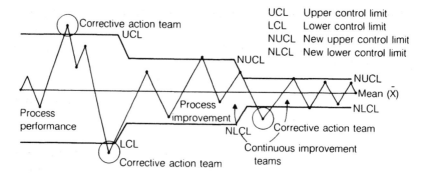

Figure 8.6 Corrective action teams and continuous improvement teams.

Coercion should not be used in the formation of continuous improvement teams. They should be voluntary gatherings of individuals usually from the same section or department. As with CATs, team size should range from between four and eight members. The leader of the team should not necessarily be the most senior individual present. The group itself should be allowed to select its own leader using such criteria as breadth of experience, organizational skills or personality.

Very often there will not be one specific problem for the continuous improvement team to home in upon. A useful start to defining the role of the CIT would be to establish the following criteria:

- aims and objectives of the department/section under review;
- analysis of the key processes which apply;
- identification of the customer–supplier chain;
- establishment of measures of performance.

Where particular problems emerge during the process of examination, the CIT itself could address the problem using the methodology described earlier for corrective aciton teams or could appoint a particular corrective action team to address the issue and recommend solutions to the continuous improvement team in question.

The amount of time employees will spend on continuous improvement team activities depends on the circumstances at the time. The team should be allowed to meet for an hour or so every week.

Shift cross-over times are useful occasions for holding meetings of this nature.

Continuous improvement teams are very similar to quality circles which dominated British industry during the 1980s. Although much hyped in the West as a result of their success in Japan, they were not a universal success here. Managers hoped quality circles would happen overnight, when in fact, because of the lack of management impetus or clear focus, they did not achieve the results expected of them. The small business manager should beware therefore not to expect an immediate surge of interest by the workforce in forming continuous improvement teams. He or she should 'recommend' certain areas for CIT examination and should 'encourage' departmental heads to persuade – in the gentlest of manners – employees to get together to form continuous improvement teams. Praise, recognition, support and publicity of the work of existing CITs are the other attributes which can be brought to bear to encourage the creation of continuous improvement teams. Within a month or so the small business manager will be in a position to judge whether the team is working successfully. However, he or she should exercise patience and not expect immediate results from the continuous improvement team. Continuous improvement in itself is a long-term commitment which will gradually gain momentum.

8.8 GOOD MEETING GUIDE

Finally, in considering teamwork, the small business manager should take into account the effectiveness and value of time spent in meetings. We have already established that time is one of the most precious resources for a small business. If a team-based approach to TQM is to be adopted, then time pressures would no doubt increase. Much could be done therefore to avoid time wasting in meetings by adopting good meeting principles. All too often people spend inordinate lenghts of time in meetings which prove fruitless while in fact they could spend less but more productive time engaged in such activities and more time helping the organization achieve its TQM objectives. Good meeting practice therefore should include the following points.

- Distribute a clear agenda beforehand which includes meeting times and location.
- Agree objectives for the meeting.
- Adopt a standard format for minutes with clear action points and time periods.
- Allocate timespans for each individual topic.
- Agree on a time period within which minutes of the meeting will be produced and distributed.
- Ensure that essential equipment – flip charts, OHPs, etc., are available.
- Keep meetings to a maximum of one and a half hours duration and whenever possible convene them before lunch.
- Arrange five minute 'comfort breaks' periodically to overcome meeting fatigue or boredom.
- Discourage lateness, smoking and personal criticism.
- Encourage healthy conflict and debate.
- Make sure all meeting members contribute.
- Ensure that the meeting does not stray off its purpose.
- End the meeting on a positive note.
- Clarify action points and summarize regularly.
- Conduct a review of the success of the meeting and take corrective action to improve the next meeting.

Specimen standard minute sheets are a useful method of ensuring a uniformity of record. The example given in Figure 8.7 is a format which leaves no doubt as to who does what by when.

8.9 CHAPTER SUMMARY

- Teamwork is one of the basic principles of TQM.
- Teamwork will establish a high level of collaboration and mutual dependence.
- A company-wide common objective is a first step to ensuring that the company operates as a single team.
- The small business manager should develop good team-building skills to set the tempo for team development throughout his or her business.

MEETING MINUTES				
NAME OF TEAM:		ATTENDEES:		
DATE OF MEETING:				
VENUE:				
ACTION No	DETAILS		RESP	D/LINE

Figure 8.7 Specimen standard minute sheet.

- Teams should not be collections of disparate individuals. They should have clearly defined objectives and agreed measures of success.
- A healthy mix of skills and personalities are necessary for effective teamwork.
- Four to eight members is an ideal team size.
- When forming teams do not alienate the remainder of the workforce by regarding team members as a select elite.
- Teams go through a cycle of development which should be mirrored by the flexible leadership style of the team leader.
- Team facilitators perform an important role in monitoring the effectiveness of a team's progress but should not assume the role of team leader or dominate proceedings of the team.
- The Quality implementation team should comprise a company's management board and have overall responsibility for the success of the TQM initiative.
- Corrective action teams are formed to resolve particular issues, especially those revealed by the various Quality diagnoses undertaken as part of the planning of TQM.
- Continuous improvement teams are groups of volunteers who have come together to improve the efficiency of a particular process or activity with a view to heightening customer satisfaction.
- Do not expect continuous improvement teams to be formed of their own volition initially. Management must take the initiative to ensure their establishment and success.
- Every team meeting should observe good meeting practice guidelines to be successful.

Quality measurement and problem-solving | 9

9.1 PERFORMANCE MEASURES

We have seen already in Chapter 4 that the building blocks of continuous improvement involve the streamlining and enhancement of business processes to elevate customer satisfaction. Having recorded by the use of flowchart diagrams (see Chapter 4) all the business processes within the organization, there comes a need to establish performance measures for each of these processes. The process mapping exercise will have confirmed the current position of the organization. Performance measures will set an improvement standard for the company to aspire to. The gap between the performance standard and current performance will indicate the degree of effort required for improvement.

To establish appropriate performance measures the small business manager should adopt the following process:

1. Establish (in writing) external customers' requirements.
2. Determine the business processes and customer–supplier chain for satisyfing customer requirements.
3. Break external customer requirements down into a series of internal customer requirements running along the 'process chain'.
4. Set appropriate measures to achieve requirements.
5. Monitor progress of achievement.
6. Once measures have been achieved, set higher measures to exceed external customers' requirements (i.e achieve the 'Quality edge' as shown in Fig. 6.1).

Customer-supplier Performance assessment Date: Department: Supplier: Customer			
Customer requirements	Measurement method	Current performance	Performance targets

Figure 9.1 Customer-supplier performance measurement documentation.

As Paul Spenley states in his book *World Class Performance Through Total Quality** TQM can only operate within a 'measurement and improvement culture' whereby every activity will have a measure appended to it. Achieving such measures will be a prerequisite to customer improvement.

Figure 9.1 is an example of the documentation that can be used to set and measure performance targets. (See also Chapter 6 for case study examples of customer-supplier performance assessments).

9.2 STATISTICAL PROCESS CONTROL

One of the key elements of continuous improvement is business process enhancement. Statistical process control (SPC) is a means

*Spenley, P. (1989) *World Class Performance Through Total Quality*, London: Chapman & Hall.

of improving processes by reducing their variability. Chapter 4 established the need to record current processes as a first step in quality improvement. Once processes have been defined, the small business manager will know whether current processes are capable of satisfying customer requirements. He or she will then be able to determine whether such processes are in practice satisfying those requirements. If not then a clash occurs between the processes' capability and its actual performance.

There will be two reasons for this. Either inherent variations will be present within the process – for example, in a manufacturing context, machine variability caused by vibration, speed or temperature fluctuations – or there will be special causes of variation – for example, operator behaviour, poor raw materials, ineffective machine maintenance and so on. To bring a process 'under control', i.e. to reduce its variability, it is first necessary to distinguish special causes from inherent causes of variability. To do this the performance of the process itself must be monitored.

Using sample data gathered by control charts and histograms (see Appendix B) the variability of a particular process can be assessed. Parameters could be set to restrict variabilty (e.g. the thickness of a particular piece of metal or diameter of an aperture). Process control charts and histograms will then establish whether the process is operating within or outside the set tolerances.

Using control charts to monitor processes over time, special causes often associated with the inputs to a process identified on the control chart as breaches of the tolerance limits will need to be identified by examining the root causes of the variation. Having eliminated the one-off special causes possibly by the formation of corrective action teams, the process will be regarded as stable or in control. In other words the variation remaining, resulting from many minor random fluctuations, will be constant. The next stage will be to reduce the random variability by improving the process itself. Variations of this kind may be a result of constant factors such as poor work layout, bad lighting or the quality or age of machinery. Removing common causes will often be beyond the capability of the individual operator and will need the intervention of management. Continuous improvement teams could also be introduced to improve the overall performance of the process.

Teams set the task for process control and improvement should utilise the problem-solving tools and techniques (as described in Appendix B) for analysing processes, removing special causes and improving on the overall capability of the process itself.

Statistical process control is not only a technique for use in a manufacturing environment but can equally be used in sales, service, support and administrative areas. Every process can be monitored, from the number of rings it takes before a telephone is answered to the most complicated manufacturing operation. When introducing SPC systematically into an organization, the small business manager should not only examine the most obvious operations – drilling holes, connecting parts, processing an order – but also the less obvious processes such as typing memoranda, arranging sales visits and convening works meetings which often result in a high cost of Quality. For SPC to work not only must it have the support of the small business manager but be 'owned' by each individual employee. In this way each member of staff monitors his or her own performance and is able to take responsibility for process improvement.

9.3 BENCHMARKING

Often companies will operate in total isolation from the outside world. As we have already established, they will not spend much time in getting to know their customers, their needs and wants. Moreover they will often be oblivious to the requirements they themselves need of their own suppliers. Invariably such companies will ignore the strengths of their competitors, be ignorant of the highest standards achieved within their industry or be unaware of the 'best in class' standards being attained in particular facets of business, whether industry specific or in general.

Benchmarking was pioneered by the American multinational firm Rank Xerox in the late 1970s as a result of devastating competition by Japanese rivals in the photocopying industry.

Benchmarking answers two questions:

Are we out performing our competitors?

Are there any companies or industries that are performing well and from whom we can learn?

There are two obvious sources of answer to these questions for the small business manager. Firstly he or she could obtain information from customer surveys, where customers are asked how the company's goods or services compare to those of competitors. Secondly, the small business manager could conduct technical evaluations of competitor products (or services).

In considering benchmarking as a measure of performance, the small business manager should gain the commitment of the management team in terms of both resources and time to be devoted to the exercise. The management team in consultation with the workforce should communicate the need for benchmarking and establish fundamental areas of the business (often called key business drivers) to be selected for comparison. Companies should be identified and means of collecting information (perhaps by forming a benchmarking team) agreed upon.

We saw earlier in dealing with customers and suppliers (Chapter 6), there is a potential performance gap between customer expectations and company performance. A similar gap could be calculated

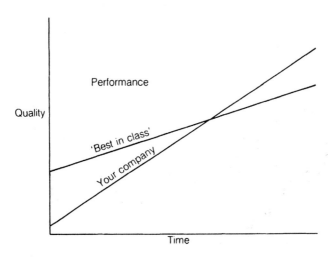

Figure 9.2 The ultimate performance goal of benchmarking is to become 'best in class'.

for current performance against the competition and the best practice irrespective of industry sector. Benchmarking will establish this (Figure 9.2).

There are effectively three categories of benchmarking:

- internal benchmarking
- competitive benchmarking
- 'best in class' benchmarking.

Taking each in turn, **internal benchmarking** occurs when one department or site within a particular organization compares its performance on a number of criteria against another site or department. For the small business manager, unless the organization is spread over a number of locations, internal benchmarking will have a limited application.

Competitive benchmarking is a more realistic proposition. In this, one company will analyse its performance in relation to a direct competitor. This exercise is probably of greatest importance to the small business manager as ignorance of the standards achieved by competitors could pose a life-threatening situation to the business.

'Best in class' benchmarking is where, irrespective of industry sector, the highest standards in business are examined. For many small business managers the difference in performance achieved from 'best in class' companies may prove startling.

To commence benchmarking, the small business manager must understand his or her own business processes. Talking to other companies about how they do things will prove fruitless if the small business manager does not know how his or her own organization functions and what its strengths and weaknesses are. The next stage in the process is to form a partnership with other companies. Information on various processes and standards will be compared and information exchanged. (Figure 9.3 gives an example of a useful 'checklist' for competitive benchmarking purposes.) Very often the small business manager will find that benchmarking partners will freely exchange information. The value of this information, in addition to the more surreptitious steps of asking customers directly and undertaking product

120

Product Comparison Form		
	Your company	Your competitors

Target markets
Benefits offered:
  1.
  2.
  3.
Quality
Price
Location
Delivery
Follow-up service
Availability
Convenience
Reliability
Service
Guarantees
Others (specify):
  1.
  2.
  3.		

Figure 9.3 Example of a check sheet for use in competitive benchmarking.

evaluations described earlier, will be to set the standard for the small business to aspire to.

Western businesspeople on trade missions to the Far East are often surprised at the amount of information imparted by their Japanese counterparts. When asked why so much information on their approach to TQM and the like is being disclosed, the ominous response of the Japanese is 'we know you will not do it'.

One final point – the size of the organization does not necessarily determine the highest standard. Some of the very smallest businesses compensate for what they lack in resources through flexibility allowed by size and can often 'set the pace' in business performance.

Case study: Benchmarking

A small adventure centre of some 35 full-time staff, with the aid of financial grants from the European Union, embarked on an extensive programme of expansion. In doing so, it extended its residential accommodation considerably and also constructed new dining facilities. To extend its appeal to a wider range of clientele, accommodation and restaurants were built to a much higher standard. The centre also intended to improve the Quality of its cuisine and recruit more staff. The centre's management team, however, was somewhat daunted at the prospect not only of accommodating and catering for a larger number of guests but also guests who were more demanding and sophisticated in their tastes and expectations.

It was suggested that some ideas on customer care, catering management and good housekeeping could be learned from some of the well-known hotel chains, many of whose customers would be potential new customers for the centre. Contact was made with a large hotel belonging to a well-known chain and ideas were exchanged. In particular the hotel's standards of customer care and catering were explained as well as its systems of kitchen management, hotel cleaning, staff recruitment and appraisal. In return the adventure centre agreed to display within its customer information documentation details of both the facilities available from the hotel contacted and details of the hotel chain's locations throughout Europe.

The performance standards procured from the benchmarking exercise gave the centre management team an understanding of the gap between its own performance and that of the hotel chain. It enabled the adventure centre to take action to satisfy the standards expected of its new customers.

9.4 THE PROBLEM-SOLVING CYCLE

In the previous chapter the continuous improvement process of TQM was embodied in corrective action (CATs) and continuous improvement (CITs) teams. For these groups to be successful, two prerequisites are required:

- an understanding of the various problem-solving tools and techniques available;
- a logical approach to problem-solving and continuous improvement.

For some reason it seems that human nature requires people to 'do something quickly' when faced with a problem. When a problem arises, managers usually dive into activity without clarifying or analysing the problem in hand. As a result problems are not resolved or the wrong problems are resolved which inevitably results in a considerable waste of effort and feelings of frustration.

A standard approach to problem-solving is encapsulated in a logical sequence – **Define** – **Analyse** – **Correct** – **Prevent**, summarized in Figure 9.4. The following sections describe each step in detail.

Define

Define the problem or issue under consideration. The team should reach a consensus as to what exactly is the problem. Some steps that will help in the defining process will include agreement on the end result to be achieved and what will be the indicators of success. The team could construct an outline plan of action and build into it particular milestones to record progress. Information that may prove of use in problem definition could include a relevant business process flowchart, details of existing procedures or a process model for the issue under examination.

Analyse

Analyse the root cause of the problem. In the analysis stage data can be collected form a number of sources using various

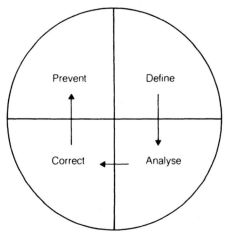

Figure 9.4 The problem-solving cycle.

techniques. Some basic analytical questions to ask would include the following.

- What data do we need?
- Where can we get it?
- How can we get it?
- How long do we gather it for?
- How do we display it?

The answers to these questions will vary according to each particular problem. A cost of Quality analysis (see Chapter 5) of the problem area will also be of use in giving a monetary value to the matter being considered. Brainstorming will help create possible root causes. Methods of data collection could include the use of check sheets, tally charts, pareto analysis and cause and effect analysis, all of which are described in Appendix B. The small business manager should ensure that this stage is not merely skated over. Without sufficient information, correcting problems and preventing their reoccurrence will be less easy to achieve.

Correct

Take action to resolve the problem. In correcting a problem it is important to focus on the root causes revealed during the analysis stage. The team should take into account all possible solutions. Paired comparison and list reduction techniques (see Appendix B) will help in prioritizing possible solutions. Pilot studies could be arranged to experiment with potential solutions. The team should then be in a position to recommend to management the most appropriate course of action.

Once implemented the success of the preventive action may be monitored by a further cost of Quality analysis to assess the reduction of failure costs. Other obvious indicators of success would include the effect of the corrective action on internal and external customer satisfaction and the effect on the company's profit and loss account.

Prevent

Prevent future occurrence of the problem. A number of measures can be undertaken to prevent future occurrence of the problem. Communicating the results of the team, standardizing related procedures and the undertaking of staff training in new methodologies are sound preventive measures. Prevention can be sustained by monitoring and publicizing results and benefits, e.g. communicating cost of Quality savings, on a regular basis. In this way staff will feel proud of the improvements in progress made.

9.5 THOUGHTS OF THE JAPANESE

The small business manager in coming to terms with TQM will no doubt come into contact with Japanese concepts and thinkers. The Japanese are past masters at error prevention and problem-solving and therefore merit some reference when considering Quality measurement and problem-solving. (Cause and effect diagrams used in problem-solving and their inventor Kaoru Ishikawa are described in Appendix B.)

Genichi Taguchi and Shingeo Shingo are two others worthy of mention. Taguchi is a Japanese engineer who popularized a particular methodology now known as 'Taguchi methods' to improve Quality and reduce costs through 'Quality engineering'. Taguchi encouraged the undertaking of Quality improvement only as long as the benefits to customers outweighed the cost of improvement. He developed the concept of 'loss' to society whereby any variation of customer expectation about a particular product or service caused a loss to the organization in money, customer goodwill and ultimately market share.

Taguchi places great emphasis on the Quality of design of a product or service so that when it is launched on the open market it will operate right first time rather than have to be perfected through a process of fault correction after launch. New models of cars, for example, should not have to be tested by the public to identify hidden faults. Taguchi advocates the testing of new products under varying conditions during the process of design so that undetected faults do not reach the customer. He also considered that an 'acceptable level of Quality' let customers down. By setting high and low tolerances for a particular product, there existed an underlying assumption that the customer would accept inferior quality. To reduce variation to a minimum Taguchi advocates the use of statistically planned experiments to distinguish between the design elements which do and do not influence its characteristics or performance. In this way error prevention and improvement activities can be channelled in a manner that will affect product Quality.

Unfortunately a book of this nature cannot do justice to Taguchi's theories, but Appendix C does give sources of further reading for the small business manager to pursue.

The second Japanese mentioned above, Shingeo Shingo, is famous for his 'Poka-yoke' system of problem identification and prevention. Shingo advocated the use of 'checklist' devices in any production process to highlight mistakes caused by human error. He recognized that people are fallible and occasionally forget things which can cause a problem further down the production line. By introducing checks at every stage, often built into production machinery, employees could ensure that any defects overlooked could be rectified, preventing errors from occurring. Shingo also advocated the adoption of source inspections – in other words examining the sorts of defects which give rise to product errors. If defects can be identified at source, then defective goods will not be produced. On a production line, if an error is identified, the production line stops and immediate feedback is given to the individual originating the error. It is corrected to allow production to continue in a defect-free manner.

Shingo's Poka-yoke system can be readily applied in a small business context. Further reading on the subject is referred to in Appendix C.

9.6 CHAPTER SUMMARY

- Process mapping will enable performance measures for each process to meet customer requirements.
- A company's performance can be estimated by benchmarking its performance against others.
- Statistical process control is a method of establishing the capability of each process in meeting customer requirements.
- Special causes of process variability can first be eradicated and then process improvement can be applied to inherent variabilities.
- In addressing problems adopt the 'Define – Analyse – Correct – Prevent' formula.
- The Japanese have excelled at problem resolution and error prevention. The ideas of Shingo and Taguchi in particular are well worth considering in depth.

Quality management systems (BS 5750/ISO 9000)

10.1 INTRODUCTION

No doubt the small business manager will have come into contact with the Quality standard BS 5750 or its European and International equivalents EN 29000 and ISO 9000. It is a standard which endorses a company's Quality management system and is designed to improve business processes and to assist continuous improvement. It is applicable to both manufacturing and service organizations alike.

Despite its benefits, many hold the negative view that BS 5750 has been forced on companies by large customers without any resultant improvement in the Quality of the supplier organization. Others consider it a bureaucratic quagmire which stifles initiative and flexibility. Companies that have been faced with this compulsion have often had to deploy hard-pressed resources to gain registration to the standard with few tangible benefits arising.

Its place within TQM is described in detail in Chapter 2 when considering the background to Total Quality. In this chapter I will describe the main stages in achieving the standard, its value to the small business manager as part of TQM, and when to apply to an external accrediting body.

10.2 BACKGROUND

The two World Wars are to a large degree responsible for the modern-day BS 5750 accredited Quality management system.

Governments during the war years, in the face of shortages of resources, placed ever-increasing pressure on suppliers – especially ordnance suppliers – to produce Quality goods. Reliability and uniformity of component parts for weaponry were of paramount importance. After the Second World War reliability and Quality standards were not relaxed. The British government produced a Quality standard for its defence suppliers – the DEF STAN 05 Quality standard series, subsequently followed by the NATO AQAP series.

The year 1979 saw the introduction of BS 5750. It was designed to rationalize various schemes being adopted by the defence industry and to transfer their benefits into the wider commercial sector. The international ISO 9000 standard was produced in 1987 for the same purpose as BS 5750. To avoid multiple assessments of suppliers ISO 9000 and BS 5750 were made identical. A further standard EN 29000 (also identical to BS 5750) was subsequently produced and adhered to in Europe.*

10.3 DETAILS OF THE STANDARD

For assessment and registration purposes BS 5750 is split into a number of parts depending on the nature of the business. Part 1 is intended for companies that engage in design and development, production, installation and servicing operations. If an organization designs and manufactures a product (or designs and delivers a service) to a certain specification, then Part 1 of the standard is the appropriate choice. Where design is not an element of a company's operations, then BS 5750 Part 2 is more appropriate. In other words, Part 2 applies to companies that produce to a customer-supplied design or an established range of products which the customer purchases as 'catalogue items'. Companies which customize products or services made to established design principles should also apply this part of the standard. BS 5750 Part 3 concerns companies solely engaged in inspection and testing operations, while a separate scheme exists for stockists of BS 5750 manufactured goods.

* At the time of going to print (June 1994) further refinements are in the process of being introduced. The new British Standard will be known as BS EN ISO9000 (w.e.f. 1 July 1994). The main changes will facilitate its use in all organizations irrespective of company size or industry.

Element	BS 5750 Clause		
	Part 1	Part 2	Part 3
1. Management responsibility	4.1	4.1	4.2
2. Quality system	4.2	4.2	4.2
3. Contract review	4.3	4.3	-
4. Design control	4.4	-	-
5. Document control	4.5	4.4	4.3
6. Purchasing	4.6	4.5	-
7. Purchaser supplied product	4.7	4.6	-
8. Product identification and traceability	4.8	4.7	4.4
9. Process control	4.9	4.8	-
10. Inspection and test	4.10	4.9	4.5
11. Inspection measuring and test equipment	4.11	4.10	4.6
12. Inspection and test status	4.12	4.11	4.7
13. Control of non-conforming product	4.13	4.12	4.8
14. Corrective action	4.14	4.13	-
15. Handling, storage, packaging and delivery	4.15	4.14	4.9
16. Quality records	4.16	4.15	4.10
17. Internal Quality audits	4.17	4.16	-
18. Training	4.18	4.17	4.11
19. Servicing	4.19	-	-
20. Statistical techniques	4.20	4.19	4.12

Figure 10.1 Comparison of requirements for BS 5750 Parts 1, 2 and 3.

131

There are nine key areas to address when considering BS 5750:

- the organization itself
- sales order entry
- design management
- procurement
- process planning
- manufacture
- inspection, test and examination
- packaging, storage and distribution
- installation and operation.

The system itself has a total of 20 quality responsibilities. Part One of the standard requires adherence to all 20 elements. Adherence is less so in Parts 2 and 3 as shown in Figure 10.1.

10.4 QUALITY SYSTEM DOCUMENTATION

In gaining accreditation every company must produce and adhere to certain documents. The first of these is the Quality manual. Its purpose is to define the company's overall policies in relation to its Quality management system. The document will be the subject of scrutiny by external assessors and customers as well as being available to every member of staff. The Quality manual need not be a large document but should be written in such a way as to be easily understood by both staff and customers.

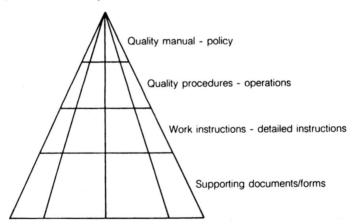

Figure 10.2 The documentary 'architecture' of BS 5750.

A second document, the procedures manual, defines the operating procedures of the company which should equate to the relevant parts of the standard. The third element – work instructions and related documents – are the detailed instructions of operations of the company. They are often combined with the Quality procedures manual.

This hierarchy of documentation is summarized in Figure 10.2.

10.5 GAINING REGISTRATION

There are a number of steps to registration as described in Table 10.1. For companies in the United Kingdom initial contact must be made to the British Standards Institute (see Appendix D for details).

There are a number of accreditation bodies that will make an assessment of the organization against the standard. Many accreditation bodies, for a charge, are prepared to undertake a pre-assessment audit to ascertain whether the organization contemplating BS 5750

Table 10.1 The 12 steps to registration under BS 5750

1. Review the company's Quality-related systems to determine the extent of compliance (or non-compliance) with the relevant part of the standard.
2. Prepare an implementation action plan estimating the time and resources required to complete all listed tasks.
3. Develop and document the quality management system to include:
   - a Quality policy manual
   - a Quality procedures manual
   - work instructions
   - applicable documents.
4. Define the Quality-related responsibilities of the directors and managers within the company, redefining the organization structure as appropriate.
5. Implement all additions and changes to existing systems and procedures and ensure compliance through staff training.
6. Introduce secure or designated storage and quarantine areas within the company's facilities through physical reorganization and/or labelling of certain areas.
7. Train selected staff in Quality auditing.
8. Select the most appropriate accreditation organization.
9. Conduct an optional pre-assessment audit by the chosen organization.
10. Correct any resulting non-compliances.
11. Undergo a full assessment audit.
12. Gain registration.

registration needs to undertake additional work before independent assessment is worthwhile. The accrediting body assessor will perform the assessment on the date specified and will be particularly concerned to identify non-conformances against the standard. Non-conformances fall into two categories – major non-conformances and minor non-conformances. The former, if uncovered, will result in the company not being awarded registration as this will represent a fundamental breach of the standard. Minor non-conformances, as long as they are not excessive, will not usually prevent a company from achieving registration as long as they are corrected within a given time period. Once registration has been achieved, external audits – usually twice yearly – will take place by the accreditation body to ensure continued adherence to the standard. If major non-conformances are uncovered during such audits, registration will be withdrawn.

In choosing an accreditation body, some such as BSI offer assessments to a wide range of businesses. Others are specific to a particular industry (e.g. TRADA Technology which is specific to the timber industry) or have high international recognition. Choice of registration body would be for the small business manager to make personally. Some of the accreditation bodies available are listed in Table. 10.2.

Table 10.2 Some BS 5750/ISO 9000 accreditation bodies

- BSI Quality Assurance Services
- Bureau Veritas Quality International
- Det Norske Veritas
- Lloyds Register Quality Assurance
- TRADA Technology
- Yarsley Quality Assured Firms

10.6 MARKETING QUALITY ASSURANCE (MQA)

Marketing Quality Assurance is an organization responsible in the UK for assessing the quality of a company's marketing, sales and customer assurance departments. The MQA specification is in line with BS 5750, and on gaining registration the organization in question is able to register its sales and marketing department to BS 5750 Part 1.

The requirements of the standard include:

- the creation of a quality policy;
- the existence of current business plans containing clearly stated marketing inputs;
- a well defined company organization stating the responsibilities and authority of staff concerned with Quality;
- the appointment of a management representative;
- a review process to maintain the continual suitability and effectiveness of the organization;
- the formation of a documented Quality system;
- marketing and sales plans;
- a code of professional conduct relating to sales and marketing activities;
- measurement systems of marketing and sales performance against plans;
- customer assurance procedures;
- purchasing procedures;
- staff development and performance measures to implement marketing and sales plans;
- controls and procedures;
- Quality records;
- Quality audits.

MQA may be a subject of interest to the small business manager with a large sales or marketing operation as BS 5750 *per se* does not cover an organization's sales and marketing activities. Application for registration to this standard will be made by approaching Marketing Quality Assurance Limited (see Appendix D for details). A pre-assessment visit and report will take place, followed by a formal assessment and, if successful, registration. As with BS 5750 registration to the standard will also entail an ongoing programme of surveillance. MQA also includes a separate special coverage for companies operating exclusively within the service sector.

10.7 COLLABORATION OF EFFORT

A particular difficulty facing the small business manager is the resources required to achieve BS 5750. Many small businesses have achieved success through flexibility and informality. Procedures are very often not recorded. Individuals have a number of different roles which are not clearly demarcated. Indeed, in many instances, employees of small businesses have not experienced a wide range of different employers and will not have been exposed to the Quality systems of other organizations. Many small bsuinesses cannot afford the luxury of a full-time quality manager who would oversee the gaining of BS 5750. Matters become worse where unscrupulous or partially skilled consultants are engaged offering a 'magic formula' for achieving the standard.

In some countries, governments grant-aid the use of consultants which for many organizations, especially in the United Kingdom, has been the favoured route to achieving registration to the standard. Nevertheless real problems of lack of time or resources still persist – especially for very small organizations perhaps with under a dozen employees in total. In such cases perhaps the most practical solution is for a number of small businesses to pool their resources and collaborate in achieving the standard. A reputable consultant could be engaged in this manner whose costs would not be inordinate as they would be shared. Each organization could then collectively go through the process to registration learning from the experiences of each individual member of the group on the way.

If a management consultant is to be engaged, or perhaps the services of an experienced Quality manager loaned possibly by one of the organizations' major suppliers, a steering committee, ideally comprising all the small business managers taking part in the consortium, could be formed to define a plan of work. Taking into account that some of the group may have already made some headway with BS 5750, some of the initial pitfalls experienced would be avoided by others in the group. The consultant or Quality manager will have to liaise closely with the steering group which will need to meet on a regular basis throughout the project.

The initial diagnostic stage, where current systems are examined and the amount of work necessary to bring systems up to the

BS 5750 standard is calculated, should not take an inordinate amount of time. British government grants for such work have sponsored up to 15 consultancy days per company, which in most cases is more than enough to undertake the work necessary. Beyond this point most small organizations take between six to twelve months before they are in a position to invite external assessment. The consultancy involvement beyond the diagnostic stage will be a matter for the group to decide bearing in mind the costs and resources involved. My advice, however, would be to continue the services of the consultant wherever possible as without such advice the burden placed on each of the small businesses involved may be even greater.

10.8 CHAPTER SUMMARY

- BS 5750 is a British Standard for quality management systems. It is identical to its International (ISO 9000) and European (EN 29000) counterparts.
- BS 5750 was first published in 1979 and harmonized with the European and International standards in 1987.
- BS 5750 is in three parts covering organizations which design, manufacture (or provide service), inspect and test.
- The standard has 20 Quality system responsibilities.
- Documentation comprises a Quality policy manual, a procedures manual and work instructions and supporting documents.
- In the UK application must be made to the British Standards Institute to gain registration.
- A number of accrediting bodies exist, most of whom will arrange for a pre-assessment review.
- External assessment will examine conformance to the standard.
- Further – bi-annual – assessments will be undertaken once accreditation has been achieved.
- Marketing Quality Assurance is an organization responsible for the registration of a company's marketing function.

- Gaining BS 5750 will assure customers that a company is practising a consistent Quality management system.
- Collaboration between a number of small companies operating in a similar field may be one solution to implementing BS 5750 where insufficient resources are available.

Investment in staff | 11

11.1 STAFF EMPOWERMENT

A small business manager's most valuable asset is his or her staff. Through a lack of resources, talented people are often very difficult to attract. Best use of what the small business manager has to hand must therefore be made. A particular problem encountered is that the management team has the authority to implement change but is very often ignorant of the problems and impediments of the day-to-day functioning of the business. On the other hand employees are all too aware of such problems but do not have the authority to change them, although they very often know exactly what needs to be done. The concept of empowerment involves granting individuals and teams within an organization the authority to resolve issues affecting their daily work. It is based on the premise that the person most knowledgeable of a particular task or process is the individual whose job this involves. The same individual, if allowed the means is best able to make improvements. The benefits of such an approach will be to instil into the workforce a sense of pride in the Quality of their work.

To achieve the enormous potential benefits of staff empowerment, the small business manager together with his or her managerial and supervisory staff must change their behaviour. Segregation between managers and staff in terms of 'brains' and 'hands' should be dispelled. In accordance with the Theory Y school of thinking (see Chapter 7) managers should trust their staff to exercise good judgement and create the conditions for them to resolve such issues. Staff must be encouraged to adopt a questioning attitude to everything they do, asking the questions 'Is this activity necessary?' and 'Is this activity cost effective?'

With an 'empowered' workforce, the role of manager becomes one of coach, advisor and coordinator, bringing together individuals from different areas of the business, where appropriate, to address cross-functional problems which occur through defective work processes or poor communications and understanding.

The small business manager can undertake a number of practical steps to empower the workforce. Firstly he or she could ensure that all of the managers and supervisors subscribe to the changing role of management, whilst being sensitive to the difficulties some 'old-school' managers will have in changing attitudes which have become entrenched over many years of experience, persevering with persuasion and personal example. The use of corrective action teams and continuous improvement teams represent a way of commencing the empowerment process.

Other practical steps would include the introduction of a 'single status' culture into the organization. Management and staff dining facilities, for example, should not be segregated. All staff, where practicable, should be encouraged to use the same entrance and exit to the place of work. The traditional privileges enjoyed by management grades should be broken down for example, avoid special parking places in the works car park and adopt a 'first come first park' rule. Set aside, say one hour's 'Quality development time' per week for the workforce either in continuous improvement teams or individually to experiment with improvements to their work. Wherever possible implement all suggested improvements even if they only have a marginal effect on the business. Another means of empowering staff to improve the business would be to establish 'ideas parties' where in a convivial setting, after working hours, staff are encouraged to meet with the small business manager to discuss the business. The only proviso for attending such events is that each individual must bring along at least one idea for improvement.

In terms of attitude, adopt Deming's maxim of 'driving out fear' from the workforce. Treat mistakes and problems as learning opportunities. Publicize any successful outcome that has occurred from a particular mistake. Finally capitalize on the loyalty of the staff and treat them with respect.

11.2 QUALITY TRAINING NEEDS

We have already established in previous chapters that the education and training of the whole organization is of vital importance. Such education and training starts at the top of the organization with the senior management team. In many cases the senior managers will insist on thorough training and education of their workforce but will not undertake the training required themselves. This will have a disastrous effect on the implementation of TQM. The workforce will have new techniques and new ways of thinking instilled in them. They will look towards their senior managers and find no change in their particular behaviour or approach to the business. The result will be that staff will 'go through the motions' but will not practise effectively the introduction of TQM. Cynicism will fester, commitment will founder.

The small business manager reading this book should by now realize that education and training starts at home. All too often in my experience managers have behaved in a way that implies that they do not need training and education but, rather patronizingly insist, that their workforce do. We have seen so far (Chapters 6 and 7) that leadership and team-building skills are of vital importance. The small business manager should establish with his or her team early on that they themselves must all behave in a manner which encourages high quality work where praise and recognition are used as the means to stimulate better performances. Such a view equally applies with even the very smallest of businesses. In organizations employing, say, under ten staff, education and training is no less important. However, the benefit within a small organization is that the whole workforce can manageably engage in such activities at more or less the same time.

An immediate difficulty in all training and education activities is finding the time without threatening the operations of the business. In-depth residential training is perhaps a luxury that few businesses could afford both in terms of cost and time. Some organizations, especially retail businesses, open their premises an hour or so later on a particular day of the week to enable the workforce to undertake training. This could be a possible approach for very small businesses whereby the telephone could be manned to take messages and explain to customers what is happening. An alternative would be for the small business manager to ask the staff for suggestions on how the issue of training and development should be addressed whilst still running the business effectively.

The use of an external resource will be an inevitable necessity at some stage during the education and training stage of TQM. Obviously cost as well as capability will be a factor in obtaining the appropriate resource. However, it is worth bearing in mind that if an external consultant is to be used then capability must be the most appropriate criterion to apply. (The use of consultants is discussed fully in Chapter 13.)

11.3 AN ANALYTICAL APPROACH

The first step in an analytical approach to the training and development of staff will be for the small business manager to become personally immersed in the philosophy of TQM. Only then will he or she be able to 'inspire' the workforce in a way that will establish TQM successfully. The reading of this book and other literature on the subject will be a good start. There are a number of one- or half-day seminars on the subject of TQM run in Great Britain, for example by the Department of Trade and Industry, the Industrial Society, chambers of commerce and local Training and Enterprise Councils, which are relatively inexpensive to attend. The small business manager may be able to take one or two of the management team to such events, or – better still – a few members of the workforce. An approach to planned reading, attendance at awareness events and the use of external training advisors are a decision for each and every small business manager to decide personally.

Once the small business manager and his or her immediate team are aware of the concepts of TQM and are fully 'signed up' to it, the education of the rest of the workforce will be an immediate next step.

Most organizations at this stage introduce external trainers. This is undoubtedly the easiest option, but it is not necessarily the most appropriate course of action. A better way, whenever practicable, would be for the senior management team of the organization to actually conduct the education and training programme themselves, leading awareness workshops and demonstrating their commitment to TQM. Initially such training could take the form of introducing the basic concepts of TQM. If each member of the management team in its role as the Quality Implementation Team has been allocated an area of TQM to champion within the organization, such individuals, following their own initial training in their chosen subject, could then follow up the initial awareness sessions with a phased introduction of training.

If the business is of sufficient size, training could be cascaded down the tiers of management, so that supervisors are trained by their managers, who in turn train chargehands who in turn train the remainder of the workforce. If such a cascade is decided upon it is important to bear in mind that the more senior managers should not divorce themselves from the lower levels of training. They should actively participate without dominating such events – again to demonstrate the importance the organization places upon such matters.

If the small business manager decides upon the approach outlined so far it is important that he or she stresses the need for the active participation of the team in these training sessions. All too often there will be one of the team who is not totally convinced or who would prefer to follow his or her residual duties rather than 'waste time' sitting in on training courses which his or her supervisors can very capably deliver. This may be so in some instances, but beware the opting out of some managers under the guise of other urgent business priorities.

Facilitator training is a method adopted by many organizations. This is where an organization selects a number of individuals from across the organization to receive in-depth training in TQM, and also in the skills of facilitating the introduction of TQM. Despite the presence of facilitators, the responsibility for implementing the day-to-day training of TQM lies with line management.

The role of the Quality manager is also of great importance in coordinating the education and training programme. I have already described the role of the Quality manager in Chapter 3. He or she should personally have gained an in-depth understanding of TQM and will be responsible for the coordination of the whole training programme.

A very effective method of enlightening an organization as to the value of TQM is to invite a speaker to address the workforce on his or her own company's achievement. Very often learning from the experience of other organizations is all that is required to tip the balance towards full commitment.

Some business communities have their own Quality clubs where representatives of various organizations gather to exchange news and experiences. Such a forum, if available locally, could also be a good stimulus to create Quality 'champions' within the organization.

11.4 INVESTORS IN PEOPLE

A UK initiative which counterbalances BS 5750 by its concentration on people is the Investors in People standard (IIP). Small business managers in the UK would do well to consider this standard as part of their TQM initiative.

The essence of the IIP standard is to coordinate an organization's investment in its staff that will give real benefit in the realization of its business goals. It will develop all staff, focusing the training and development so that they have the right skills and knowledge to make a significant contribution to the success of the business. In a TQM context, IIP will not only aid the small business manager by providing a framework within which to coordinate the associated training and education activities, but will also raise the profile internally and externally of the business as an organization which truly values its staff as its most important asset. The standard comprises four points as shown in Figure 11.1.

The standard itself will be awarded by the local Training and Enterprise Council (TEC) (Local Enterprise Councils in Scotland). It will involve making a 'plan of action' to achieve the standard and the announcement of a formal commitment to the local TEC of the intention to apply for IIP. Once an organization is confident that it has achieved all the requirements of the standard a qualified assessor will be appointed to examine a portfolio of documentary evidence substantiated by on site interviews with the management team and their employees. A written report will be submitted to the TEC for consideration. The TEC itself will award IIP status to successful organizations.

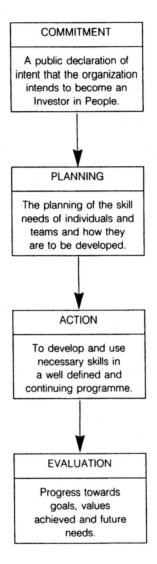

Figure 11.1 Investors in People.

As with BS 5750, IIP status will be subject to re-assessment – in this case every three years. Evidence of the continuing development of the workforce will need to be supplied if recognition as an Investor in People is to continue.

145

11.5 PERFORMANCE APPRAISAL AND REWARD

There has been a considerable amount of debate concerning whether performance-related pay (PRP) is compatible with TQM. Traditional systems of PRP promote the achievement of individual objectives. The argument runs that by promoting the individual, teamwork – one of the foundation stones of TQM – would be undermined. In the case of a sales team, it has been alleged that in a PRP context customer care would suffer as individual salespeople concentrate on the level of sales rather than satisfaction of customer needs. Similarly a production department will focus on quantity rather than quality if working to individual objectives.

Performance appraisal is closely associated with performance-related pay. In its traditional usage it has been a system of annually or bi-annually assessing past achievements against objectives set. There will have been a heavy stress during this process on criticizing past performance, and an over-emphasis on the pay rise emerging from such an assessment.

For the small business manager considering this issue, best practice would be to design a system of appraisal which emphasizes a combination of individual Quality objectives, team contribution and behavioural style. The linkage to pay should be apparent although not direct, lest the pay element of performance appraisal 'contaminates' the effectiveness of the whole exercise.

In introducing performance appraisal, the small business manager and his or her management team should determine the company's mission and purpose. From this should emerge a series of actions which must be achieved for the organization to realize its mission. Only the organization as a whole can achieve the mission statement. A cascade effect could now be introduced depending on the size of the organization, whereby each individual manager agrees a range of objectives which are in turn broken down into individual objectives for his or her subordinates. This stage would be replicated throughout the organization until everyone in theory is working to job objectives which impact upon the company mission.

The performance appraisal system should work upon the basis of a continuous cycle. Objectives agreed should be reviewed on a six-monthly basis. The review could embrace a combination of

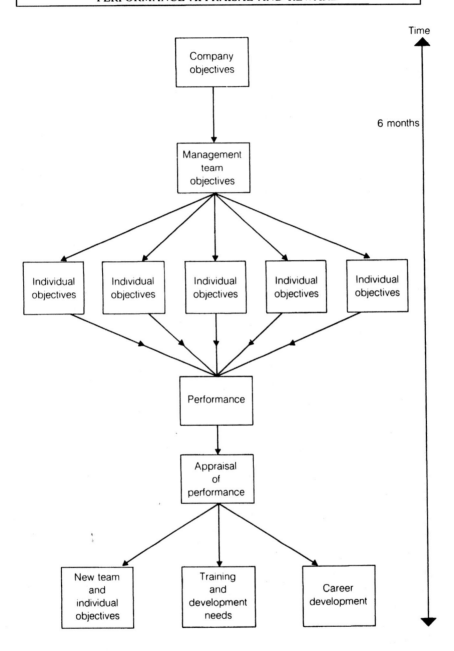

Figure 11.2 The performance appraisal process.

INVESTMENT IN STAFF

PERFORMANCE APPRAISAL   DATE:_____

PERSONAL

Name:	Job title:
D.O.B.:	Service in current job:
Service with company:	Location:

PERFORMANCE

Job task and objectives:
(As stated in job description)

Achievements	Difficulties encountered

PERSONAL STRENGTHS	HIGH	MEDIUM	LOW	NOT ACCEPTABLE
Communications - Spoken - Written				
Development of staff				
Planning of own work				
Commitment and workrate				

OVERALL ASSESSMENT (i.e. Job performance and personal qualities)		
Excellent		Comment
Superior		
Satisfactory		
Less effective		
Unacceptable		

AGREED ACTION FOR IMPROVEMENT

(Including training needs)

NEW TASKS AND OBJECTIVES

(To be included in job description)

OVERALL COMMENTS

Appraiser

Appraisee

Signed_____ _____
        (Appraiser)   (Appraisee)

Date _____ Date of next appraisal_____

Figure 11.3 A specimen performance appraisal document.

self-assessment by the individual and an independent review by the individual's superior. The result would be a comparison of assessments and agreement on performance plus a consensus on new objectives. Training and improvement strategies to make up for areas of deficiency would also occur in such a cycle. Figure 11.2 illustrates the process for the management team of a small company.

In addition to new objectives and a training and development plan, career development options may emerge from the process. Such options would attempt to cater for both the personal aspirations of the individual and be in line with the planned growth of the business.

Some further words on objective setting for individuals would include the need for objectives to be clearly understood by both parties and constructed in such a way as to be easily measurable. There is little point in setting vague objectives open to personal interpretation such as 'do a good job in production' or 'ensure the effective running of the sales team'. Only when objectives have been made explicit can job performance be measured.

By the dual approach of appraising results and behaviour, the performance appraisal system augments TQM in encouraging achievement in a manner that stimulates both individual and team effort. An actual example of the documentation associated with such an approach adopted by a small company within the construction plant hire industry is given in Figure 11.3.

11.6 PAYMENT SYSTEMS

If a company achieves a certain amount of success – say in increasing profit or sales turnover – as a result of the collective efforts of the workforce, then it would seem only fair that the workforce should share in that success by financial gain. However, as success has been achieved by the team effort of the workforce, the reward should be for team performance. In this way the payment system will encourage greater team effort and apply team pressure on poor performers to improve their work rate and cooperation. 'Gain sharing' as it is sometimes referred to has powerful motivational overtones. Not only profit or sales turnover could be used as performance targets, but also internal targets as, for example, by sharing the gains achieved from the collective cost savings to the organization through the cost-conscious efforts of the workforce.

A simple way of encouraging collective effort and sharing in the success of the business is to introduce a group bonus scheme. This could work along the following lines.

- The small business manager determines a profit target for the business. If the target is achieved a portion of such profit is syphoned into a bonus pool.
- The bonus pool is allocated amongst the workforce either pro rata to the wage of each individual staff member or as a standard lump sum payment. The first method will obviously result in higher wage earners achieving the larger bonus. In the latter a flat bonus payment will proportionately reward most those earning the least within the organization.

Some bonus schemes can be designed specifically to reward quality of product. The following case study taken from a textile manufacturer illustrates how staff can be rewarded for producing a quality product.

Case study: Quality incentive scheme

The company believes that a cooperative drive by all concerned can convert much of the seconded and rejected cloth into a higher level of first-quality fabric to an internationally accepted standard. The problems associated with high seconds and reject rates are within our control. These can be cured by a concerted team effort.

A quality incentive payment scheme is therefore to be introduced for which all staff on site are eligible. The scheme is based on metreage and percentage of first-quality cloth products inspected and dispatched.

Payment will be based on the following formula:

89% or lower in first quality = no bonus
90% in first quality   = £100.00 (half yearly)
91% in first quality   = £150.00
92% in first quality   = £200.00
93% in first quality   = £250.00
94% in first quality   = £300.00
94% in first quality   = £350.00

151

The quality incentive payment will be paid on the average first quality achieved over a six-month period, i.e. if 92% first quality is achieved during the year then total bonus would be £400.00 per employee and so on. The incentive will be paid prior to Christmas and the annual holidays, with the average taken over five months and any readjustment made at the next six-monthly payment.

On a general note, pay and conditions of service of businesses applying TQM should not be inhibiting factors. Paying an above-average basic wage will not only attract good employees but help to retain them, especially if group bonus schemes based on profitability are utilized.

11.7 DEVELOPMENT OF A SUGGESTION SCHEME

The Milliken Carpet Company, winner of the 1992 Malcolm Baldrige Award for Quality in America, has developed TQM to such a degree that on average each employee within the organization produced some fifteen suggestions per annum. Fifteen staff suggestions is more than many organizations receive per annum from their entire workforce. Toyota, one of the world leaders in staff suggestions, boasts fifty per head per annum. Both these, albeit very large, organizations have shown the commitment to TQM necessary to achieve such an impressive level of employee contribution and involvement. The small business manager can equally harness the talents of his or her own workforce by showing similar commitment.

The lifeblood of any suggestion scheme is recognition and a genuine desire on the part of the company to implement the suggestions of its workforce. Suggestion schemes traditionally have not been a great success. The principle reason for this has been management behaviour. A typical scenario would be for the management team to announce enthusiastically the reintroduction (perhaps for the third or fourth occasion) of a suggestion scheme with a monetary incentive (usually insignificant) for, say, the top three suggestions. A procedure would be developed in which staff suggestions had to pass through several ranks of supervisors and managers before reaching the suggestion committee. The committee would be made up of several senior managers (but not the managing director) with perhaps a token workforce representative. A flurry of suggestions would arrive in the first month. Many of them would be vetted out as 'part of one's normal job' or some such similar excuse. Of the smaller number eventually to be considered by the suggestion committee, two would perhaps be recognized as worthwhile, one would be implemented and the financial inducement awarded. The following month the number would reduce. By month three suggestions would not be forthcoming. This scenario, although exaggerated, is not untypical of the way many organizations treat staff suggestions. Is there any wonder that the improvements that can emerge from such schemes are untapped?

The value of staff suggestions is based on the premise that a person fulfilling a task every day as part of his or her regular job is in a far better position to know what is going wrong and to come up with suggestions for improvement. If the culture of the organization has constantly criticized and frowned upon staff doing anything apart from getting on with their job then the many many improvements that can emerge from successful staff suggestions will be lost. The small business manager should adopt the attitude 'why not implement the suggestion?' rather than the more widespread view 'why should I?' By implementing as many staff suggestions as possible, irrespective of whether they all add spectacular value to the organization or not, a message would be communicated to the workforce of commitment to and the value of the staff's contribution to continuous improvement.

To introduce a successful suggestion scheme the small business manager, as a demonstration of commitment, should attend, if not chair, the suggestion scheme committee. The committee's representatives should reflect the makeup of the company with a cross-section of committee members coming from each area of the business. All suggestions made should receive some recognition – whether it be financial or non-financial.

Winning suggestions could receive a whole range of rewards from a percentage of the savings to the company resulting from the suggestion to a mere public handshake and thank you note from the small business manager in person. The monetary sums involved

153

need not be large. Jim Maxim, the former Chief Executive of Laura Ashley, for example, introduced a 'That's dumb' campaign throughout the organization, whereby £5.00 was awarded for every procedure or working practice pointed out as unnecessary. Recognition and communication of the success of the suggestion is the essence of a fruitful suggestion scheme.

Case study: Staff suggestions

A small horticultural nursery as part of its Total Quality Management initiative introduced a staff suggestions scheme. Every suggestion was carefully examined. most were implemented. One particular suggestion involved the layout of young trees within the company's nursery fields. Up to that time saplings had been planted in a reasonably organized fashion by tractor and automatic planting equipment. Some trees would be broken by the wheels of the tractor. Odd pockets of land through their inaccessibility to the tractor and trailer would remain unused. A member of staff involved in this annual operation suggested the use of a theodolite to align the planting rows. The adoption of such a suggestion resulted in a 20% better utilization of company land and a reduction in plant loss through tractor damage by over 80%.

11.8 CHAPTER SUMMARY

- One of the small business person's most valuable assets is the staff.
- Staff often have greater insight into day-to-day problems affecting the business than a company's management. 'Empowerment' creates the conditions in a company to enable staff to address these problems.
- Where staff are empowered to improve the business, managers and supervisors must change their behaviour, acting more in a coaching and advisory role.
- Practical steps such as 'Quality development time' and 'ideas parties' can be introduced to promote the views of staff.

- Training and education in TQM is essential for all members of staff. It should cascade throughout the workforce commencing with the small business manager and his or her immediate team.
- Managers and supervisors should play an active role in the education and training of the workforce.
- Investors in People (IIP) is an external standard advocating the effective training and development of staff. Its principles adapt well to a company practising TQM.
- A system of performance appraisal could be introduced which is linked to the overall business goals, assessing not only individual contribution but also team effort and cooperation.
- Bonus and incentive schemes should be introduced to reward collective effort and to share out the financial benefits accrued by the company in practising TQM.
- A well devised suggestion scheme can unveil many potential sources for improvement. Wherever, practicable suggestions should be implemented. Rewards and recognition should be proportionate to the benefits achieved.

PART THREE

Implementation of Total Quality

TQM implementation | 12

12.1 WHERE TO START?

The purpose of Part Three of this book is to establish a logical sequence to the introduction of TQM and to give encouragement and reassurance. Figure 12.1 contains the issues which may need to be taken into consideration. Reference to each topic can be found in the main body of the text.

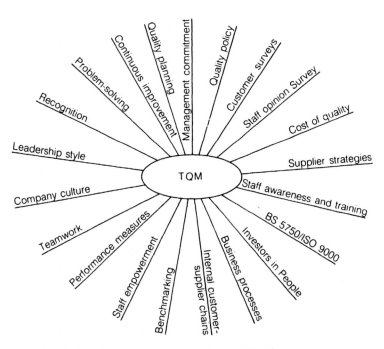

Figure 12.1 TQM implementation: matters for consideration.

159

The small business manager who has persevered so far in the reading of this book may well be disconcerted by the many themes and techniques described. He or she may be at a loss as to where to start, particularly when considering the wide range of implementation strategies put forward by the leading exponents of TQM. However, within the United Kingdom the most common implementation plans feature the elements contained in Figure 12.2. For the smaller business some of these elements may have a ring of 'getting ready to get ready'. Whilst commitment, analysis and planning are essential, there must be a balance between long-term goals and short-term benefits for the small business. Indeed the small business manager may well have been adept at some elements of TQM for many years. Moving forward on a broad front with continuous improvement is a luxury the small business can ill afford.

The best method of making progress is to select certain themes for improvement. By re-focusing on new themes as success is achieved, the full implementation of TQM will, in time, be covered. The advantage to the small business is that results will come quickly, which in itself will gain the commitment of the workforce and sustain the momentum. Small businesses notice improvements in performance much sooner than larger businesses and success can be demonstrated very quickly. The following two case studies illustrate how small businesses can achieve early results.

Case study 1

Company A – a small manufacturing firm

This company, a manufacturer to the automotive industry employing some 40 staff, experienced considerable material wastage and delays to its delivery schedules which had recently upset a number of its customers.

To tackle these issues a cost of Quality analysis of the company was undertaken, involving the whole of the workforce, together with an analysis of business processes. Everyone in the company was involved in this exercise. The rationale for such activities were explained beforehand to deflect any suspicion of improved efficiency being equated in the minds of staff

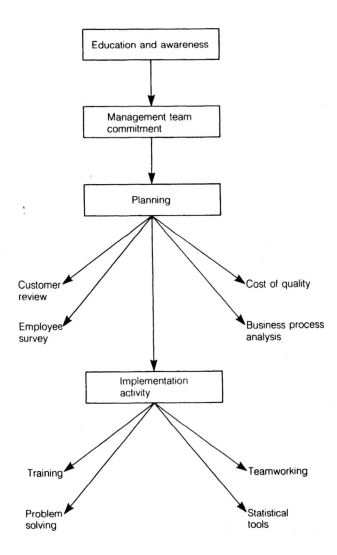

Figure 12.2 A typical TQM implementation plan.

161

with job cuts. As a result an accurate picture of the organization's operations was obtained which enabled corrective measures to be undertaken involving the streamlining of processes and the reallocation of duties. As a result the company was able to reduce both scrap levels, improve employee performance and increase customer satisfaction.

Case study 2

Company B – a small professional services organization

A long established organization providing professional services to the local business community suffered a reduction in revenue caused by the loss of a number of its long standing customers to a newly established rival company. To meet this threat, the organization in question undertook a comprehensive survey of its customers. The results produced many surprises, a number of which were unpleasant and unexpected.

Acting on this information the organization refocussed its activities, realigning its services to the expectations of its customers rather than for its own convenience. As a result customer relations with its existing clients improved and a number of new customers were gained.

The remainder of this chapter deals with the elements of TQM implementation in greater detail.

12.2 UNDERSTANDING AND COMMITMENT

The first step to successful TQM is a thorough understanding of the subject. There are many sources of information. Extensive reading, attendance at seminars and talking to other organizations are all sources already referred to. Without a thorough understanding of TQM the small business manager cannot sound convincing to others. Leading by example will demonstrate commitment.

As already stated, Western management all too often goes through the motions of commitment, cheerfully delegating the responsibility of TQM to others whilst fulfilling their part as and when called upon. Such an approach is certain to fail. Maybe there will be some partial success initially, but without sustained commitment and demonstrable practice the potential benefits of TQM to such an organization will not be realized to any great degree. TQM must be seen as the most important priority for the small business manager if he or she expects it to be adopted by the rest of the company. Again, depending obviously on the size of the small business, the small business manager must ensure that the management team also shows commitment before expecting the workforce to take up the practice.

12.3 GETTING THE MANAGEMENT TEAM ON BOARD

The first problem presenting itself to the small business manager is how to get the immediate team of managers to share his or her commitment. As in the case of the small business manager, understanding is the precursor to commitment. The ease of management team commitment will depend to a large degree on the size of the organization in question. In a business of under 25 employees the small business manager may consider it more worthwhile to address the issue of commitment for the whole workforce in one fell swoop. Larger businesses with an established management structure will make such a strategy confusing and impracticable.

The leadership qualities (discussed in Chapter 7) of the small business manager will certainly help to achieve the necessary 'buy in'. A powerful approach would be for the small business manager to share his or her own personal understanding and commitment with the team. At a management team meeting the small business manager could announce his or her understanding of TQM and its appropriateness for the business, attend seminars with his or her managers *en bloc* or select a few members of the team and attend such events together. Others could visit neighbouring companies to share their experience. In other words each individual member of the management team could be allocated specific fact-finding tasks and report back. The shared experience of learning should act as a powerful stimulus.

Commitment cannot be demanded of others. Individual interviews with each member of the management team will establish for the small business manager whether every member of the team is 'on board'. At such interviews the small business manager will have the opportunity of impressing upon colleagues his or her own commitment and be able to instil a sense of urgency into each individual.

12.4 PLANNING THE IMPLEMENTATION

Despite the temptation to rush forth into action, the planning stage of TQM remains a crucial step. What the small business manager must attempt with his or her team of managers is an implementation plan which embraces the whole organization. Chapters 3, 4 and 5 have already covered in depth these aspects of self-examination. In summary only 'hard' information gained from customer and staff surveys, and business process and cost of Quality analyses, can establish the base point for progress. The implementation plan itself will establish the company's destination and means of arrival. Performance measures will act as milestones on the way. Mission statements, quality policies, clear job descriptions and clarity within the role of the management team are all important aspects of the planning stage.

The forming of a Quality implementation team with allotted responsibilities for each management team member to 'champion' will aid the development of the plan. Involvement of the workforce could commence at this stage. The enthusiasm of the small business manager and his or her team should be communicated. Ideas and areas of concentration should be encouraged from everyone. Regular updates should be communicated via the establishment of a system of team briefing. Progress reports and successes (and failures) should be disseminated in a controlled fashion.

Once the plan has been established, some general awareness training could be introduced to the workforce as a whole. If time is of the essence TQM presentations could be made during the lunch periods or for brief periods after work. However, TQM training should not be made a burden for staff. It will soon become a turnoff if it means regular late evenings at work. Figure 12.3 gives an example of a TQM implementation plan for a small business in flow chart form.

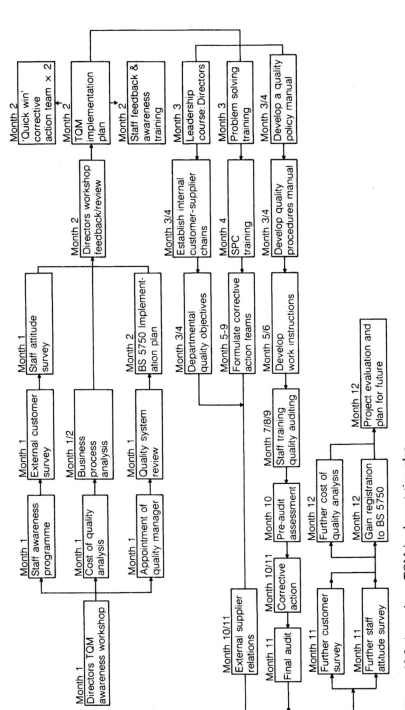

Figure 12.3 A specimen TQM implementation plan.

12.5 'QUICK WINS'

As shown in Chapter 8 in discussing corrective action teams, there is nothing like early succss to reinforce commitment. The small business manager should chose some short-term improvements which are relatively straightforward to enact. Form a corrective action team, train it in problem-solving techniques, update the remainder of the workforce on progress and reward success. Choice of 'quick wins' could ideally tackle an issue which has for some time been a source of aggravation for the workforce which will produce immediate benefits once addressed. Issues such as improving the accuracy and speed of overtime payments or improving the paper flow within a particular bottleneck endured by everyone are typical 'quick wins' adopted. It should be remembered, however, not to chose a problem that will prove inordinately complex and time consuming to solve or where a successful solution is very much in doubt.

12.6 SUSTAINING COMMITMENT

The most difficult aspect of TQM is long-term sustained commitment. The small business manager must personally exercise self-discipline and perseverance. Only his or her own strength of character will be able to sustain the motivation of others. Times will no doubt arise when the small business manager will be tempted to abandon Total Quality. When faced with such a prospect he or she should weigh against the high percentage of failures through lack of sustained commitment, the enormous benefits to be gained from perseverance.

In time and with determination Total Quality should become self-propelling. One of the greatest motivators for the workforce is to see progress. Statistical process control charts showing improvements, or run charts showing profit increases or cost of Quality reductions, should all be given a high profile within the company and should be displayed in such a way as to be clearly visible to all.

Once the workforce has adopted TQM work will become more enriching. A fundamental change in company culture will have occurred whereby the excellence of an 'empowered' workforce is achieving success and reward.

12.7 REVIEW

However, despite the fact that the company may have adopted TQM with enthusiasm and is achieving results, complacency should be avoided. As stated earlier there is no real destination to TQM. Its philosophy is one of continuous, never-ending improvement. At regular intervals (e.g. three monthly) review meetings of the Quality implementation team should be held over and above the regular progress meetings. During these reviews measures set down within specific time periods should be appraised. When measures have not been met, amended plans should be formed. Each manager championing his or her particular area of TQM should be accountable for achieving specific measures set out at the planning stage.

At the six- or twelve-month stages of TQM implementation, the small business manager should hold an overall review of progress. The most effective way of doing this would be by holding further staff and customer surveys and a further company-wide cost of Quality analysis. Information gained from these sources will highlight further measures for improvement.

To complement improvements the real indicators of success which make Total Quality a worthwhile exercise are the improvements to overall company performance. Market share, profitability, return on capital employed or increased sales will act as the real indication of success.

12.8 CHAPTER SUMMARY

- When implementing Total Quality it is important to balance long term goals with short term benefits.
- Understanding and commitment are essential prerequisites to the successful implementation of TQM.
- An early task for the small business manager is to ensure that the team of managers share his or her commitment and understanding.
- Planning must take place before action. It should be based on 'hard' evidence of current performance.

- During the planning phase, the workforce as a whole should be made aware of the impending change and be educated in TQM principles.
- 'Quick wins' using corrective action teams to resolve issues that are not difficult to overcome and have a universal benefit should be implemented to give the TQM drive initial impetus.
- Sustained commitment is all-important to make TQM a success.
- Visible displays of TQM improvements will serve as a stimulus to greater effort on the part of the workforce.
- Regular reviews of progress should be held and amendments to the implementation plan introduced where necessary. Overall reviews should be held at the six-month and twelve-month stages of TQM implementation.
- Increased sales turnover, profitability, market share and return on capital employed will be the real indicators of success.

Final thoughts

13.1 SOME DO'S AND DON'TS

By way of introduction to this final chapter I have included a number of one line dos and don'ts which will act as an *aide-mémoire* to the small business manager to avoid the obvious pitfalls which may be experienced on the journey to Total Quality. They are not in any specific order and should be referred to as a checklist to ensure that the principles unfolded in this book are being adopted.

Dos

- Lead by example.
- Engage external help where necessary.
- Accept ultimate responsibility for TQM.
- Develop a new attitude towards people.
- Make TQM the number one priority.
- Sustain commitment to TQM.
- Establish a single-status company.
- Join a Quality club.
- Use mistakes and customer complaints as opportunities for learning.
- Communicate TQM progress (including setbacks) to the workforce.
- Encourage teamwork.
- Become thoroughly versed in TQM principles.
- Visit companies practising TQM.

- Recognize and reward success.
- Be patient.
- Be positive.

Don'ts

- Use slogan campaigns.
- Offload responsibility for TQM onto someone else.
- Rush the implementation of TQM.
- Disregard the customer's needs.
- 'Revert to type' when faced with setbacks.
- Expect quality to 'just happen'.
- Concentrate on quality management systems like BS 5750 in isolation.
- Restrict TQM just to the working environment.
- Give up.

13.2 GROUPS AND SOCIETIES

I have already referred to the benefits of a number of small organizations acting in collaboration. An additional source of mutual support and help can be obtained from a number of groups and organizations. In addition to government industry departments, many chambers of commerce and Training and Enterprise Councils organize Quality forums to pool thoughts and experiences of TQM. The Industrial Society in the United Kingdom (see Appendix D for details) run a number of 'Quality clubs' throughout the country, designed to stimulate debate, share experience and develop practical action plans for implementing Total Quality. In Wales, the Wales Quality Centre also has a similar remit. On a European-wide front the main body is the European Foundation for Quality Management (EFQM). Its role is to strengthen European industry through a focus on TQM. To become a member organization a company must be based and registered in Europe. In addition to the publication of materials and the arrangement of seminars, the EFQM presents an annual quality award to the most successful exponent of Total Quality, together with a number of European Quality prizes for demonstrable excellence in TQM. In addition to a useful source of information, membership of the EFQM will be a source of help to companies who trade within the wider European market. (The address and telephone number of the foundation is contained in Appendix D.)

13.3 USE OF CONSULTANTS

Ever since Robert Townsend in his book *Up the Organization** said that the management consultants 'borrowed your watch, told you the time and charged you for it,' consultancy has enjoyed a mixed reputation. Stories of inflated fees and luxury-style expenses add to many people's trepidation. For the small business manager without unlimited resources or experience of their use, the hiring of a consultant to aid the introduction of TQM is a considerable decision.

Consultants can fall into two crude categories – 'the expert' and 'the facilitator'. The expert will give all the specialist advice necessary and will draw on vast experience gathered over many years. The facilitator, a process consultant, whilst being knowledgeable in the field, will exercise his or her skills in more of a counselling role to assist the introduction of change. Fee income can vary in the UK from £250 to £2,500 and above per day, so it is important that the small business manager exercises caution before reaching for the business services directory.

It is important first of all to examine the particular types of consultancy firms available. Like the building industry they range from the sole practitioner to firms of world-wide standing with annual fee income well in excess of many large multinationals. In more detail they could be categorized according to size in the following sections.

Sole traders

These are often retired senior managers with a wide variety of business experience. They can be of two types – the all-round generalist able to give business advice on a number of fronts, or the

*Townsend, R. (1984) *Up the Organization*, London, Michael Joseph.

specialist with detailed expertise in a particular field. Sole traders may operate within a network whereby other independents with particular skills may be called upon to give a specialist input as and when necessary. In terms of fees they can vary according to reputation and ability, from a couple of hundred pounds to well over a thousand pounds per day. Usually, however, their charge rates are at the lower end of the fee scale.

Niche consultancies

Sometimes called 'boutiques' because of their specialist range of wares, niche consultancies are the next size up to the sole traders. These are specialist firms proffering consultancy services on a narrow front. Such firms may specialize in marketing, corporate recovery, corporate tax or career counselling. Many TQM consultancies fall into this category. Such firms may be localized to a particular area or be spread over a number of locations both nationally and internationally. Some may be 'splinter groups' of larger organizations. Companies which often engage consultants have in recent years made considerable use of niche firms, using them as precision tools to tackle a particular problem. As with the sole trader fees vary according to reputation. In general, however, their fee rates are higher than individual operators.

Academics

In line with the spirit of enterprise, the business schools of many academic institutions offer consultancy on the side. Some such institutions have built up considerable reputations and when acting in a consultancy capacity bring to bear considerable depth of experience. Consultancy assignments using academic institutions will often involve a combination of formal training at the particular institute augmented by on-site assistance. Fee income will again vary but in general falls in the middle or lower ranges of the scale. One caveat when contemplating the use of academics: check that their academic pedigree is matched by their 'hands-on' experience.

Plc consultancies

Some large organizations have commercialized their own internal consultancy resources to operate on the open market. IBM and ICL, at one time, would be examples of the so-called Plcs. Their advice tends to reflect the main line business, whereby their considerable degree of 'in-house' expertise is exploited externally. Fees for such consultancies will depend on the organization in question.

Mainstream consultancies

These are organizations which concentrate on management consultancy services alone. Size varies but usually they are medium to large organizations with a wide range of specialisms. Such firms are nationally, if not internationally, based and often operate at the large company end of the market. They will have established an impressive track record and will be able to bring resources to tackle most issues arising in client organizations. Fees usually are middle to high. Many large companies make use of such firms, often engaging them to implement major change programmes across international frontiers.

Accountancy firm consultancies

These are the 'big brothers' of the consultancy world. The international accountancy firms have huge resources at their disposal. They style themselves as 'one stop shops' and can provide the full panoply of business and consultancy services from business start-ups to corporate recovery. They are often structured into specialist units under the overall supervision of a generalist partner who can put together a team of specialists to cater for every need. The fees of such firms are usually high, particularly when senior or highly specialized members of the organization are called upon.

Surveying such a 'beauty parade' must cause the small business manager some consternation. Before considering guidelines on whom to engage the small business manager must weigh up the advantages and disadvantages of introducing consultants to assist with TQM. The advantages of a consultancy intervention would include:

- the injection of expertise not present within the organization;
- experience of the pitfalls encountered by similar businesses;
- a source of impartial advice and objectivity and a person company employees will be able to confide in without fear of personal redress;
- a person likely to advise the small business manager of potentially costly mistakes.

The disadvantages of consultants include:

- the danger of the small business manager offloading his or her responsibilities onto an independent third party;
- if the wrong consultant is engaged, bad advice may be given that will have a detrimental effect on the organization;
- advice may be over-prescriptive or 'off the shelf' rather than tailored to the needs of the particular client organization;
- an accommodating client may be sold further services not necessary for the development of his or her business;
- they may be regarded as a threat or an executioner by managers and staff;
- high cost.

Without being totally impartial, I would advise all small business managers coming to grips with TQM to consider seriously the use of good TQM consultants. The right person can save the small business manager both time and money in advising on the most appropriate route to take, pointing out the pitfalls on the way. When engaging a consultant, unless it is for a specialist piece of work of a finite nature, such involvement should be tapered, with a heavy input at the beginning of the assignment gradually decreasing over time as the small business manager and his or her team gain in confidence. Thereafter, consultants can be usefully retained on a care and maintenance basis, being called upon at particular points during the TQM process to review progress and advise of future steps.

One important point to stress when using consultants is that the process changes resulting from the consultant's presence are 'owned' by the small business manager and his or her company. Consultants should not be used as convenient scapegoats in the face of reluctance, and equally they should not be endowed with the responsibility for change.

To close this section I have drawn up a checklist to help the small business manager decide upon consultancy help.

- Invite a number of different consultancy firms to discuss the issues at stake and submit a written proposal on how they would intervene.
- State the requirements clearly and the desired outcome. Include the preferred timetable for the completion of the assignment before inviting written proposals.
- Ensure that any proposal includes a comprehensive programme of work, and exact inputs, timings and costs, together with the 'deliverables' from any assignments.
- Beware of package solutions which may not cater for the particular needs of the business.
- Ask for reference sites of previous consultancy engagements of a similar nature and contact the companies given.
- Make sure that you are not confronted by a mere 'sales team'. If those presented to you are concerned with business development ask to meet the actual consultants who will be undertaking the work before reaching a decision. Request the curricula vitae of consultants to be used. Quiz them on their ability and experience.
- Ask colleagues within the local business community and government business and enterprise agencies to recommend consultancy organizations of repute. The Association of Quality Management Consultants, the British Quality Association and the Institute of Quality Assurance are useful contacts (see Appendix D) as they maintain a register of approved Quality consultants.
- Take care to clarify the business expenses associated with the use of consultants and agree an expense budget beforehand.
- Request itemized invoices for work undertaken.
- Agree the procedure for any changes in the assignment part way through or if the consultant engaged falls sick or leaves the consultancy firm.
- Agree a formal contract for the work.
- Finally, do not select a consultant on cost alone. Chose a consultant whom you and your colleagues are comfortable to work with.

13.4 QUALITY OF LIFE

Total Quality above all is an attitude of mind supported by planning, application and simple problem-solving techniques. It is strange, however, to find that people practising such principles at work do not necessarily adhere to the same codes of conduct out of work. If the small business manager and his or her staff have become truly committed and convinced that TQM is the first priority at work, why not adopt the same principle in all spheres of life?

The 'Define–Analyse–Correct–Prevent' sequence to problem-solving could easily be adopted in our home life. Home maintenance, garden management, personal finances to give but three examples could all be tackled more effectively using the DACP cycle. Teams existing outside work – the family, the social club, sporting organizations – could all benefit enormously if the principles of teamwork described in Chapter 8 were adopted. A customer conscious attitude could be developed towards people we provide for in a social capacity. One's personal health and fitness could be a subject for TQM. Weight loss or reduction in cigarette smoking and alcohol consumption could all benefit from the use of SPC techniques. Major new personal projects like mastering a foreign language or playing a musical instrument are two examples of major undertakings people spend their time engaged in and very often fail at because of a lack of the same sustained commitment which results in so many failures of TQM at work.

Advocates of TQM will have a heightened sensitivity for customer satisfaction in their domestic lives. They will not endure poor service whether from a bank, a garage or a supermarket.

Indeed TQM should be applied to our treatment of the environment both as individuals and as a community. Reductions in the waste of vandalism and the expense to us as taxpayers in reparatory work or unnecessary prevention measures should have a considerable personal and community-wide benefit. Communities in the United Kingdom, for example the 'Quality North Campaign', and in the United States where many communities have initiated their own TQM progrmames are just some examples of where TQM is taking root outside work. Within a Social Services concept citizens' advocacy

176

is now in evidence. Volunteers under the guidance of Social Services authorities act on behalf of the infirm or aged members of the community. The UK government's 'Citizen's Charter' – a policy designed to improve public services – has four aims all akin to TQM principles:

- to work for better quality in every public service;
- to give people more choice;
- to make sure everyone is told what kind of service they can expect; and
- to make sure that people know what to do if something goes wrong.

Empowerment, giving individuals responsibility for improving their working lives, could easily be transferred into the community obviating the need for excessive state controls and coercion. 'Ownership' of one's destiny and collective responsibilities, although a far cry from the life we find in our inner cities for example, may as we pass the millennium become a reality.

If Total Quality is to become all-pervasive, as now seems likely, then the small business manager of the future will not see his or her company operating in a TQM vacuum. It will be just one entity in a much wider Total Quality process.

Appendices

Appendix A
Glossary of terms

Accepted Quality level (AQL) The proportion of units within a batch which meet customer requirements. An agreed AQL will mean that the customer is prepared to accept a certain number of defective items.

Appraisal costs The checking and inspection costs undertaken by an organization to ensure that its product or service meets customer requirements.

Basic operational costs The costs an organization cannot avoid encountering during the normal performance of its business.

Benchmarking A means of comparing a company's own performance with the recognized leader within a given business sector or across industry and commerce.

BS 5750 The British standard designed to ensure that organizations establish and maintain a Quality management system.

Cause and effect diagram Another name for the fishbone or Ishikawa diagram.

Common cause An inherent flaw within a particular process causing random variation of output.

Continuous improvement team (CIT) A voluntary group from the same work section meeting regularly to improve a particular process or operation.

Control chart A chart with upper and lower control limits drawn to plot the performance of a particular output or activity.

Corrective action team (CAT) A work group under the leadership of the local supervisor formed to solve a particular problem.

Cost of conformance The costs an organization incurs in meeting the requirements of its customers.

Cost of non-conformance The costs incurred by an organization in repairing what has gone wrong in meeting customer requirements.

Cost of Quality The sum of the costs of everything that would not have been necessary if everything else was done right first time.

Empowerment A concept whereby individual employees are given authority to resolve the day-to-day issues they experience in their working lives.

EN 29000 The European Quality management system standard equivalent to BS 5750 and ISO 9000.

External failure costs The costs incurred by a company of things going wrong once the product has left the organization.

Failure mode and effect analysis (FMEA) A technique to uncover and eliminate potential faults within a product design or process.

Fishbone diagrams Also known as cause and effect or Ishikawa (after its originator) diagrams. A problem-solving technique used to identify the relationship between causes and effects.

Flowchart A chart using established symbols to portray diagrammatically how a process works.

Histogram A means of displaying the frequency distribution of the quantitative variation of a particular characteristic.

Inputs Materials or services received from a supplier (internal/external) which enables a work activity to take place.

In-process inspection The inspection of goods or services during the process of manufacture or service provision against a set specification.

Internal failure costs Costs incurred by a company when things go wrong before the product or service has reached the customer.

Investors in People (IIP) A UK standard to enable companies to train and develop their staff effectively.

Ishikawa diagrams See Fishbone diagrams.

ISO 9000 The international standard for a Quality management system equating to BS 5750 and EN 29000.

Just in time A system of material control used to ensure minimum stocking and effective delivery to the right place at the right time in a production process.

Kanban The Japanese system of just in time management.

Kaizen The Japanese system for continuous improvement.

Mission statement A pattern of words which encapsulates a vision of the success and future direction of an organization.

Non-conforming item A Quality assurance term which states that a particular product or item does not meet the agreed specification.

Outputs The products or results of a particular process.

Paired comparisons A group technique of prioritizing items on a list without incurring problems of voting.

Pareto analysis A means of differentiating the 'critical few' causes of a problem from the 'trivial many'.

Poka-yoke A method designed by Shingeo Shingo for mistake-proofing processes by the introduction of checklists along a production process.

Prevention costs The costs incurred by a company in preventing its goods or services from not meeting customer requirements.

Process A sequence of activities which produce an output or result from the transformation of inputs through the controlled application of resources.

Process capability The range of inherent variability of a process in operation.

Process control A means of maintaining the variability of a process within the pre-set limits.

Process mapping A technique for recording diagrammatically, using flowcharts, the way a process works.

Quality The satisfaction of agreed customer requirements.

Quality assurance The systems and planned activities that assure customers that a product or service meets specified requirements.

Quality control The means of ensuring that a product or service meets Quality requirements.

Quality implementation team The senior managers of an organization allocated with the responsibility for leading the implementation of Total Quality.

Quality manager A person designated with the coordination of the day-to-day activities associated with implementing TQM.

Quality manual A document defining a company's overall policies in relation to its Quality management system.

Quality planning Activities to ensure that Total Quality is introduced in an effective manner.

Quality policy A statement of a company's Quality intentions stipulating rules, responsibilities and priorities.

Quality procedures The day-to-day procedures which a company enacts in adherence to its Quality management system.

Requirement A description of an input or output to a process.

Root cause The underlying reason for an occurrence.

Statistical process control (SPC) A range of statistical techniques for monitoring and improving the performance of a process.

Supplier An individual (internal or external) who supplies goods or services to a customer specification.

Total Quality The mobilization of the whole organization to achieve Quality continuously and efficiently.

Taguchi methods A number of techniques, pioneered by their inventor Genichi Taguchi, to ensure that a product or service was designed in such a way that when launched on the open market it would operate right first time.

Zero defects A manufacturing objective to produce defect-free products.

Appendix B
Problem-solving tools
and techniques

B.1 INTRODUCTION

Throughout this handbook frequent reference has been made to teamwork and preventive measures in the drive towards Total Quality. In this Appendix I have described the most frequent means of addressing problems that TQM teams use. Also described are various means of data collection to allow informed decisions to be made. The following questions should be asked by any team about to collect data on a particular problem.

- What information do we need?
- Where can we obtain it?
- How can we obtain it?
- How long do we gather it for?
- How do we display it?

The small business manager should ensure that he or she personally as well as members of the mangement team are well versed in the following techniques so that a general training programme could be undertaken, ideally, for all employees. The best method of becoming familiar with problem-solving techniques is to practise them regularly. After a while their adoption will become second nature within the organization.

The practice of problem-solving techniques is equally important for the small business manager and his or her management team.

If the company as a whole is expected to plan and analyse before producing solutions, then clearly this process should apply to the company's management team.

The following guide will help the small business manager select the appropriate problem-solving technique or data collection method likely to be used in the process of problem resolution.

1. **Define** the problem:

   - cost of quality analysis
   - business process analysis
   - staff survey
   - customer survey
   - Gantt charts.

2. **Analyse** the problem:

   - checksheets
   - histograms
   - flowcharts
   - run charts
   - pareto analysis

3. **Correct** the problem:

   - brainstorming
   - list reduction
   - paired comparisons
   - cause and effect diagrams.

4. **Prevent** the problem from recurring:

   - failure, mode and effect analysis.
   - statistical process control.

A useful aid to problem-solving would be to categorize the problem in question according to whether it is within the control of the team totally, partially or out of its control. It would be pointless for a corrective action team to address a problem which was out of its control. Figure B.1 illustrates the point.

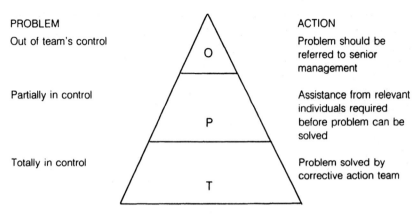

PROBLEM

Out of team's control

Partially in control

Totally in control

ACTION

Problem should be
referred to senior
management

Assistance from relevant
individuals required
before problem can be
solved

Problem solved by
corrective action team

Figure B.1 The problem solving pyramid.

In conclusion perhaps the most effective tools for any problem-solving team to use are the words 'Why?' and 'How?' Asking these questions repeatedly will often lead to the root cause of a problem or more creative solutions.

B.2 BRAINSTORMING

One of the most frequently used problem-solving tools and techniques is brainstorming. Its purpose is to generate as many ideas as possible within a group. It is a very effective method of finding the root cause of problems.

To undertake brainstorming the problem-solving group should comprise some four to eight people all of whom are familiar with the issue under consideration. The group leader should define the situation in question and then record on a flipchart the views of the group. The situation examined should be clearly defined before the brainstorm commences to ensure specific comment.

Ground rules to be followed for a successful brainstorming exercise are as follows.

- Avoid all criticism or comment within the group of suggestions put forward (however outlandish).
- Welcome quantity.

- Confine suggestions or causes to one- or two-word descriptions.
- Record everything stated.
- As team leader, build on the ideas being produced to generate further thoughts once the initial exercise is complete.

There are two basic forms of brainstorm – the 'free for all' where team members put forward ideas at random, and the 'round robin' method where each team member in turn is invited to put forward suggestions. While both methods are effective, a 'free for all' brainstorm, as long as it is well managed by the team leader, is likely to produce a better result than the alternative method which can dampen the tempo of the session and also place excessive pressure to produce something original on those team members who are last to be asked.

An example of the results of an actual brainstorm session for the issue 'Potential barriers to the implementation of TQM into a small business' are recorded in Table B.1.

Table B.1 The results of a brainstorming exercise

• Company culture;	• Bureaucracy;
• Family conflict;	• Unclear roles;
• Fear of the unknown;	• Poor quality equipment;
• Confidentiality;	• Family loyalties;
• Inability to take hard decisions;	• Fundings;
• BS 5750 pressures;	• Untrained workforce;
• Cashflow;	• Competence of management;
• Management style;	• Lack of praise;
• Absence of teamwork;	• Quality control culture;
• Excess checking;	• Lack of trust;
• Lack of management commitment;	• Unclear work processes;
• Low staff morale;	• Poor quality materials;
• Damage to equipment;	• Bad working environment;
• Time;	• Undermanning;
• Poor work flow;	• Poor customer relations;
• Ignorance of cost of quality;	• Lack of teamwork

B.3 LIST REDUCTION

Successful brainstorms, if well run, will produce a welter of ideas many of which will overlap or be impracticable to implement.

List reduction is a method of filtering such items to achieve a more manageable list.

There are a number of ways of reducing and prioritizing a brainstormed list. One technique would be for each member of the team to designate their five most important topics by numbering them five to one. The topic with the most points from the team is the most important one and should merit prior consideration to the rest.

Another method of list reduction would be to record each issue emerging from the brainstorm on a piece of paper. The team then segregates each issue into relevant families. The makeup of each family of issues is then reduced where overlap occurs or the same issue has been recorded more than once.

A third method would be for the team to agree a set of criteria to apply to each item recorded as, for example:

- Is it practicable?
- Will it cost too much?
- Can it be undertaken within a reasonable timescale?

If each item does not pass all the criteria set, then it should be removed from the list. The process of list reduction should finish when a manageable list (say ten items) has been achieved.

B.4 PAIRED COMPARISONS

This is a very useful technique for prioritizing items on a list without incurring problems of voting. Using a standard format (Figure B.2 gives an example) each team member individually records each item derived from the reduced brainstorm list. They then compare item one with the remaining items, circling which of the items compared is the more important. Then item two is compared with the remainder in a similar manner and so forth down the list. The winning scores, i.e. the numbers circled, are calculated. Each team member then records the number of circled '1s', '2s', etc., in the left-hand column of the bottom matrix on the form.

Once the exercise has been completed, the scores of the whole team are totalled and prioritized. Paired comparisons enable corrective

Paired comparison chart

No.   Item

1		1 2	1 3	1 4	1 5	1 6	1 7	1 8
2		2 3	2 4	2 5	2 6	2 7	2 8	
3		3 4	3 5	3 6	3 7	3 8		
4		4 5	4 6	4 7	4 8			
5		5 6	5 7	5 8				
6		6 7	6 8					
7		7 8						
8								

Vote matrix for paired comparisons

No.	Member votes														Totals		Ranking
1																	
2																	
3																	
4																	
5																	
6																	
7																	
8																	

Figure B.2 Paired comparisons.

action teams and continuous improvement teams to concentrate on the most important issues as identified by the group.

B.5 CAUSE AND EFFECT DIAGRAMS

The cause and effect diagram, also known as the 'fishbone' or Ishikawa diagram (after its Japanese originator), is an excellent means of segregating particular causes of an effect. The 'head' of the fishbone is used to record a problem, effect or desired state, while the bones of the fish coming from the central spine are given generic headings, very often the four Ms – methods, machinery, materials and manpower – or the four Ps – people, products, price and promotion. Particular causes are then drawn on the scions to the main bone structure under the relevant heading. An example of a cause and effect diagram is given in Figure B.3.

The team as a whole will allocate causes under the agreed headings. Very often this will spur the need for more information which is subsequently allocated. Causes of the problem can then be reduced in a systematic way.

Many companies place cause and effect diagrams on general display on the factory floor or in the general office. Individual members of staff are encouraged to record their own views on the causes of the effect under consideration. When this happens, the corrective action team often colour code the causes to symbolize current actions, as for example:

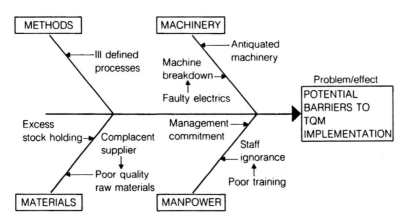

Figure B.3 Cause and effect diagram highlighting some of the barriers to TQM implementation.

Green dot   – Issue solved
Blue dot   – Issue under consideration
Red dot   – Issue irrelevant
Brown dot   – Issue not yet addressed

B.6 FORCE FIELD ANALYSIS

A useful technique for problem-solving teams is force field analysis. It is a technique used to help establish whether change is possible or desirable. Force field analysis operates on the premise that every situation is in a state of equilibrium as a result of driving forces for change being counterbalanced by forces resistant to change.

By identifying the driving and resisting forces, teams will be able to break down the resistors systematically and encourage the driving forces to remove the state of equilibrium and achieve the desired change.

The method of analysis is to list all the driving forces that would move a situation to change. Opposite this list are recorded all the resisting forces that would hinder change. Whichever list is the larger will identify the dominant factor in any proposed change, as shown in Figure B.4.

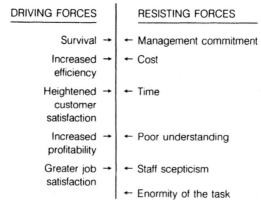

Figure B.4 Force field analysis.

194

B.7 DATA COLLECTION

One of the most important aspects of the problem-solving cycle described in Chapter 9 is the collection and analysis of data before any corrective action is undertaken. In this section I have described the most common methods of data collection likely to be required by the small business manager.

The checksheet

This is probably the most frequently used method of collecting data. Its purpose is to record the frequency an event occurs over a period of time. When gathering data in this way it is important that the data collectors are clear as to what exactly is to be observed and recorded, and also the time period for observation. A standard checksheet form should be designed and used to ensure consistency of data collection.

Using checksheets data can be collected by sample or continuous observation. Whatever method is adopted it is important to ensure that the same consistency of sampling period is used by everyone engaged in the exercise.

An example of a checksheet is given Figure B.5.

Pay queries to finance department					
Type:	Wk. 1	Wk. 2	Wk. 3	Wk. 4	Total
Change of hours	11	1	1	1	5
Overtime	11	111	1	11	13
SSP	1	11	1	1	5
Not paid		1	11	1	4
SMP	1				1
Starter's pay	1		11		3
Leaver's pay		1			1
Allowances				11	2
Tax deductions	11				2
No pay slip		1		1	2
Pension queries	1	11	1		4
					42

Figure B.5 An example of a checklist.

195

Frequency tables

The use of frequency tables is another very well known method of data recording. It is used to record variations within given tolerances of a particular event. As with checksheets there should be agreement as to the time period or the amount and frequency of the items to be checked. Thickness, weight and speed are the usual variants for which frequency tables can be designed.

An example of a frequency table is given in Figure B.6.

Thickness		Number
3.0	3.1	1
3.1	3.2	2
3.2	3.3	7
3.3	3.4	9
3.4	3.5	15
3.5	3.6	8
3.6	3.7	16
3.7	3.8	24
3.8	3.9	3
3.9	4.0	1
		86

Figure B.6 An example of a frequency table.

B.8 HISTOGRAMS

Histograms are a technique for displaying the frequency distribution of the quantitative variation of a particular characteristic. It is used to great effect when wishing to display the effect of numerical variation. Histograms can be a means of communicating effectively to staff who operate a particular process. Information gathered on checksheets or frequency tables can easily be converted into histograms and illustrate the degree of variation of a particular characteristic. They can act as a powerful motivator for improvement.

The frequency distribution of the height of a particular group of women provides the data for the example of a histogram in Figure B.8.

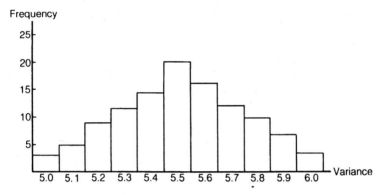

Figure B.7 An example of a histogram.

B.9 PARETO ANALYSIS

Pareto analysis is based on the principle that in any given distribution 80% of the effects are produced by 20% of the causes. Pareto analysis is a means of distinguishing the 'vital few' 20% causes from the 'trivial many'. It allows corrective action teams to focus on issues which will have a real effect once resolved. All too often managers waste time on unimportant issues, e.g. cancelling the company newspapers as a first step in an economy drive, in a semblance of progress. The use of Pareto analysis will overcome such futile activity and focus attention on the major causes of the situation under examination.

To construct a Pareto chart, first rank data collated by cause according to frequency. Then form a bar chart of the ranked frequencies of the cause. A graph can then be plotted equating to the frequency distribution.

In the example given in Figure B.8, three main causes result in the greatest frequency of typing errors. These would be the main causes for a corrective action team to focus its attention in improving typing efficiency.

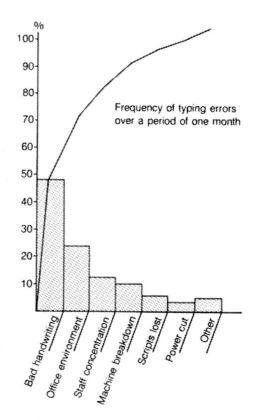

Figure B.8 Pareto analysis.

B.10 CHARTS

Charts are useful methods of displaying visual changes in processes or events over time.

198

Run charts

These are simple charts designed ot show variation over time. Their specific use is in the application of statistical process control (see Chapter 9) where tolerance levels are set and the divergence of the flow from the mid point can pinpoint the need for corrective action. A target measure can also be set as in the example given in Figure B.9.

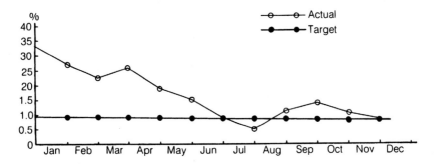

Figure B.9 An example of a run chart.

Gantt charts

A Gantt chart is a method of scheduling and assigning responsibilities pertaining to a particular project over time. When examining

TASK	RESPONSIBILITY	SCHEDULE			
		Month 1	2	3	4
1. Planning workshop	Senior management team	▨			
2. Cost of quality	Finance manager	▨			
3. Customer survey	Marketing manager		▨		
4. Staff survey	Personnel officer		▨		
5. BS 5750 Audit	Quality manager			▨	
6. Staff training	Management team/ Personnel officer			▨	

Figure B.10 An example of a Gantt chart

199

The problem highlighted can be passed via the log to the quality implementation team, who can determine the makeup of a corrective action team to address the problem. The results can be recorded on the same document and returned to its originator. Use of such documentation is one of the methods of encouraging staff to take responsibility for highlighting problem areas and for sharing in the responsibility of correcting them. Figure B.11 gives a specimen format for a problem-solving log.

B.12 FAILURE MODE AND EFFECT ANALYSIS (FMEA)

FMEA is a standard technique to uncover and eliminate potential faults within a product design or process. A standard document is recommended as in the specimen shown in Figure B.12. The use of FMEA is as follows.

1. Record the part or process.
2. List all potential failures that may occur.
3. List the likely effect of each failure identified.
4. List the causes of each of the failures.
5. Predictions must now be made on the probability, severity and detection of the failure (using a 1 to 10 scale for each factor where 1 equates to very low and 10 very high).
6. Multiply all three factors to give an improvement weighting which will indicate the priority areas for improvement.

Failure mode effect analysis

Part or process	Potential failure mode	likely effect of failure	Cause of failure	Probability factor A	Severity factor B	Detection factor C	Improvement weighting A × B × C

Figure B.12 Specimen sheet for failure mode analysis.

Appendix C
Further reading and
video selection

The following is a list of books I have either used during the course of researching this book or which I consider the small business manager may find of particular use in broadening his or her knowledge of TQM. There are also a number of periodical publications available. In the UK the Department of Trade and Industry have published a number of useful guides on particular aspects of TQM. An independent publication I would recommend is the bi-monthly *TQM Magazine* published by IFS Limited, Wolseley Business Park, Kempston, Bedford MK42 7PW.

At the end of the bibliography I have also included a number of training videos on TQM. These can be either purchased or hired for short periods and can help the small business manager in training and communicating TQM to the workforce. On average they run for between twenty and forty minutes.

TQM BOOKS

Atkinson, P.E. (1990) *Creating Culture Change: The Key to Successful Total Quality Management*, Bedford, IFS.
Bank, J. (1992) *The Essence of Total Quality Management*, Hemel Hempstead, Prentice Hall.
Crosby, P.B. (1979) *Quality is Free*, New York, New American Library.

Crosby, P.B. (1984) *Quality Without Tears, The Art of Hassle Free Management*, Maidenhead, McGraw-Hill.

Deming, W.E. (1986) *Out of the Crisis*, Cambridge, Cambridge University Press.

Fiegenbaum, A.V. (1983) *Total Quality Control*, Maidenhead, McGraw-Hill.

Hakes, C. (ed.) (1991) *Total Quality Management: The Key to Business Improvement*, London, Chapman & Hall.

Hutchins, D. (1988) *Just in Time*, Aldershot, Gower.

Ishikawa, K. (1990) *Introduction to Quality Control*, London, Chapman & Hall.

Juran, J.M. (ed.) (1988) *Quality Control Handbook*, Maidenhead, McGraw-Hill.

Lochner, R.H. and Mater, J.E. (1992) *Designing for Quality: An Introduction to the Best of Taguchi and Western Methods*, London, Chapman & Hall.

McNealy, R.M. (1993) *Making Quality Happen: A Step-by-Step Guide to Winning the Quality Revolution*, London, Chapman & Hall.

Martin, P. and Nicholls, J. (1987) *Creating a Committed Workforce*, London, Institute of Personnel Management.

Oakland, J.S. (1986) *Statistical Process Control*, London, Heinemann.

Oakland, J.S. (1989) *Total Quality Management*, London, Heinemann.

Peters, T.J. and Waterman, R.H. (1982) *In Search of Excellence*, New York, Harper & Row.

Pike, J. and Barnes, R. (1994) *TQM in Action: A Practical Approach to Continuous Performance Improvement*, London, Chapman & Hall.

Popplewell, B. and Wildsmith, A. (1988) *Becoming the Best: How to Gain Company Wide Commitment to Total Quality*, Aldershot, Gower.

Price, F. (1990) *Right First Time: Using Quality Control for Profit*, Aldershot, Gower.

Quinn, F. (1990) *Crowning the Customer: How to Become Customer Driven*, Dublin, O'Brien Press.

Rothery, B. (1991) *ISO 9000*, Aldershot, Gower.

Shinego, S. (1986) *Zero Quality Control – Source Inspection and the Poka Yoke System*, Stamford, Conn., Productivity Press.

Spenley, P. (1992) *World Class Performance Through Total Quality*, London, Chapman & Hall.

Wilson, G. and Miller, R. (1990) *Taguchi Methodology within Total Quality*, Bedford, IFS.

TQM VIDEOS

Crosby on Quality (two videos), BBC, London.

Ideas Unlimited, BBC, London.

I'll Know When I See It, Gower Training Resources, Aldershot.

In Search of Quality Volumes I and II (four videos), Video Arts Limited, London.

In The Customer's Shoes, Melrose Film Productions, London.

Journey to Excellence, BBC, London.

Making Customer Service Happen, Melrose Film Productions, London.

Managing Customer Service, BBC, London.

Quality Circles – Involvement At The Point Of Work, Gower Training Resources, Aldershot.

Quality In Practice: BS 5750 – Making It Work For You, BBC, London.

Quality In Practice: Kaizen – The Art of Continuous Improvement, BBC, London.

Quality – The Only Way, Melrose Film Productions, London.

Quality – Why Bother?, Video Arts Limited, London.

Stuck On Quality, Video Arts Limited, London.

The Customer Is Always Dwight, Video Arts Limited, London.

The Tom Peters Experience – The Customer Revolution, BBC, London.

Total Quality Management (seven videos), Melrose Film Productions, London.

Your Place In Total Quality, Longman Training, Harlow.

Appendix D
Useful addresses and sources
of further information

Association of British Certification Bodies
2 Park Street
London
W1A 2BS
Tel: 0171-495 4193

Association of Quality Management Consultants Limited
4 Beigne Road
Olivers Battery
Winchester
SO22 4JW
Tel: 01962 64394

British Deming Association
2 Castle Street
Salisbury
Wiltshire
SP1 1BB
Tel: 01722 412138

British Quality Association
10 Grosvenor Gardens
London
SW1W 0DQ
Tel: 0171-823 5608

British Quality Foundation
Vigilant House
120 Wilton Road
London
SW1V 1JZ
Tel: 0171-837 8600

British Standards Institute
Enquiry Section
Linford Wood
Milton Keynes
MK14 6LE
Tel: 01908 221166

European Foundation for Quality Management
Building Reaal
Fellenoors 47a
561AA Eindhoven
Holland
Tel: +31 40 461075

Industrial Society
Robert Hyde House
48 Bryanstone Square
London
W1H 7LN
Tel: 0171-262 2401

Institute of Quality Assurance
10 Grosvenor Gardens
London
SW1W 0DQ
Tel: 0171-401 7227

Irish Quality Association
Merrion Hall
Strand Road
Sandy Mount
Dublin 4
Eire
Tel: +353 1 269 5255

Marketing Quality Assurance Limited
Park House
Wick Road
Egham
Surrey
TW20 0HW
Tel: 01784 430953

National Society for Quality Through Teamwork
2 Castle Street
Salisbury
Wiltshire
SP1 1BB
Tel: 01722 326667

Peratec
Nottingham Road
Melton Mowbray
Leicestershire
LE13 0PB
Tel: 01664 501501

Quality Methods Association
Meeting Point West
6a St Marys Bridge
Plymouth Road
Plympton
Plymouth
PL7 4SR
Tel: 01752 348358

The National Quality Information Centre
PO Box 712
61 Southwark Street
London
SE1 1SB
Tel: 0171-401 7227

Wales Quality Centre
QED Centre
Main Avenue
Treforest Industrial Estate
Pontypridd
Mid Glamorgan
CF37 5YR
Tel: 01443 841381

Index

Page numbers appearing in **bold** refer to figures and page numbers appearing in *italic* refer to tables.

211

Printed in the United Kingdom
by Lightning Source UK Ltd.
117674UKS00002B/36